WHAT DID JESUS DO?

Becoming Like Jesus in Teenage Years and Beyond

EVAN CHRISTOPHERSON

ISBN 979-8-89043-740-2 (paperback)
ISBN 979-8-89043-741-9 (digital)

Christian Faith Publishing
832 Park Avenue
Meadville, PA 16335
www.christianfaithpublishing.com

Printed in the United States of America

To my beautiful wife, Haley, and my precious daughter,
Zoe. I love them more than they'll ever know.

To my parents, Steve and Leslie Christopherson,
who raised me to love Jesus. What a gift.

To the current and former students of Clearpoint Church.
All glory to God for the time we've had together.

CONTENTS

FOREWORD

I have had the privilege of knowing Evan Christopherson since his birth. I am honored to be his father. He has had a special love for and relationship with the Lord his whole life. Surrendering to full-time ministry at church camp his sixth grade year, he never looked back. Evan took education seriously and graduated summa cum laude from Houston Baptist University with a degree in Christianity, then immediately pursued and completed a master's in Divinity by age twenty-five. Although Evan made straight A's, he passionately studied to fully embrace the knowledge found in God's word. During this time, he worked as a youth pastor and a junior varsity baseball coach for the Homeschool Christian Youth Association. I was blessed to watch him marry his wonderful and supportive wife, Haley, a Houston Baptist University graduate, and have their daughter, my granddaughter, Zoe!

Evan has already established an impressive and productive career as a youth pastor. He began as a part-time youth pastor for a small church in Pearland, Texas, before he was called to be the student pastor of Clearpoint Church. That ministry has thrived under his leadership, and his youth group has not only grown in number, but also spiritually. Many of his youth go on to serve in youth or other areas of the church after graduation. He has a gift in being able to bring the knowledge he received from getting his masters of Divinity and bringing it to a level where students can understand. Evan preaches with a passion and urgency that ignites in people the desire to learn more. He is able to relate with students and adults on a level that breeds a connection that lasts throughout life. Evan understands the pain and pressure that today's youth are facing. He is an expert in connecting youth experiencing today's pressures with the path that Jesus walked. He stays firm with the scriptures and reveals the truth of God's Word at all times.

Evan has several years of experience as a youth pastor. With a bachelor's degree in Christianity and a masters of Divinity, he is definitely qualified to write *What Did Jesus Do?* What I find most interesting is that, although it seems to be written for teenagers, adults will find just as much value reading this book as anyone. One only needs to browse the table of contents to realize this book has a wealth of knowledge for even the most seasoned Christian reader. I am most excited to use this book in my practice as a Christian psychotherapist that works with adolescents. I was appointed by Governor Perry to the Texas State Board of Examiners of Licensed Professional Counselors and became chair of the same board by Governor Abbott. During my eleven years working for the State of Texas, I found, time and time again, the need for counselors to have a resource like *What Did Jesus Do?* I feel certain this book will be a great help to counselors across the State of Texas and the nation. One often hears that teens need a great role model. As someone who was teaching high school in 1981 and continues to work with adolescents, I am confident this is *the* book to point them to the Jesus that understands their struggles. I am certain every reader will find a greater value and appreciation for Jesus after reading, *What Did Jesus Do?*

Steve Christopherson
MS, LPC, NCC, CEO of Pro-Act Counseling

INTRODUCTION

The way we live matters. Not so that we can earn salvation or earn grace from God. Those things can never be earned. Scripture is clear that grace is a gift. The gift of salvation creates a desire in the hearts of believers to glorify God and live in a way that is pleasing to him. Time and time again, the call of the scriptures is to be holy as God is holy. In 1 Peter 1:15–16, Peter writes, "But just as he who called you is holy, so be holy in all you do; for it is written: 'Be holy, because I am holy.'" Hebrews even says that without holiness, no one will see the Lord (Heb. 12:14). The way we live matters, because God is holy, and he's called us to that same level of holiness! We must also realize that the decisions we make will shape the trajectory of our lives. Every day, we are faced with things that we can control and things that we cannot control. Regardless of what we face, we will always have opportunities to make decisions with the circumstances that arise, and making the right decisions can be extremely difficult at times. It can be difficult to know what the right decision is, or sometimes, we just don't *want* to do the right thing.

I remember a time when I found myself in a little predicament. It was late one Friday night. I was fifteen years old, and as you know, most fifteen-year-olds stay up pretty late on Friday nights, especially when friends are staying over. When you combine the natural energy that teenagers have with the amount of Red Bull we drank, we knew it would be about three thirty or four o'clock in the morning before we went to bed. We spent most of the night playing a man-hunt-type game that we had made up around the neighborhood. We would spend hours playing this game, and it was always so fun! I would still be up for a game now as an adult! On this particular Friday night, the game ended around 2:15 a.m. My friend and I headed inside, and we were winding down watching some TV. But my brother Ean and our other friend weren't ready to call it quits yet. They stayed outside for another thirty minutes or so. Around two forty-five, they came in and tried to talk us into going back out to play some more games. Truthfully, I was tired and ready to fall asleep. But I decided I would go back out because there are only so many Friday nights in a teenager's life to do this type of stuff.

Once we were outside, the four of us started walking around the block when one of our friends who stayed outside the whole time decided that he was gonna go ding-dong ditch one of the houses. I know this is hard to do these days since all of the doorbells have cameras on them, but that's probably for the best. My friend was fearless and didn't really seem to think through the consequences or the fear that would be entering the homeowners. When he made his move to go ring the doorbell, the other three of us took off running. But I did turn around to watch, and unbeknownst to me at the time, this friend had already ding-dong-ditched these people two times that night. I found out the hard way, because as he went to ring the doorbell, the door opened. It was at this moment that I realized how weak our friendship truly was. Because even though I was pretty sure he was about to be dragged into the house and possibly tortured (okay, that probably wasn't going to happen), I only ran away all the faster. The remaining three of us decided to go hide on the side of a house. Thankfully, we were at our friend Bubba's house. So even though we were in a little bit of a predicament, we could at least feel a little bit safe with the fact that we were good friends with the kid who lived there.

The sense of peace did not last long. It was moments after we made it to the side of Bubba's house that we began to see flashlights and hear footsteps. It was obvious that if we stayed where we were, we would be found easily. We made the decision to jump Bubba's fence and hide in his backyard. And boy, did we make it just in the nick of time. Because no sooner did we make it over the fence than the people with the flashlights passed by. We felt a sense of relief being protected by the fence, but we also felt nervous, because the homeowners seemed persistent on finding us. We watched them go back and forth a few times. Each time they walked by, I got more nervous. We hid in the backyard of Bubba's house until around 4:00 in the morning. And then things took another turn. Bubba's back door opened.

I knew right away that it was Bubba's dad drinking coffee and getting ready for his Saturday morning shift at work. We were still on the side of the house so he couldn't necessarily see us. To say that I was in a situation where I didn't know what to do is an understatement. But we knew that we couldn't stay there. The funny thing about the whole thing is that I know Bubba's dad. In fact, I was friends with Bubba's dad. He was and still is a cool guy. But I don't know how cool he is at 4:00 in the morning with kids in his backyard without his permission. And the risk of him hearing us or walking over and seeing us seemed too great. We knew it was time to jump the fence again and make a run for it.

We quietly snuck back over the fence and formed a game plan. I told my brother and our other friend to follow my lead. The plan was to sprint across the street as fast as we could. If we could make it to the house across the street, we could jump their fence. The beauty behind that would be that my house was the house behind that one. So we were essentially two fences away from being home free. I whispered a countdown from three, and we took off as fast as we could go. Once we were in the middle of the street, a flash of light hit my face. I heard the man yell, "Hey! Stop!"

Of course, this only skyrocketed our adrenaline and made us run even faster. As we approached the five-foot chain-link fence, I think the Holy Spirit came over me. I jumped in the air and did a dive roll over the fence without ever touching it. Yes, I have witnesses. To this day, I honestly think it was one of the coolest things I've ever done.

The three of us made it over both fences, and we were inside hiding in our room, praying that we wouldn't hear a knock on the door from the police. Being under my blanket never felt so good. But that night was filled with a lot of temptation, peer pressure, fear, anxiety, confusion, and even anger. Yes, I was angry at my friend who ran to ring their doorbell in the first place. By the way, he talked to the police, and all they told him was to stop doing it and they sent him home.

The truth is, that awful night (which is actually funny to look back on now) is a pretty accurate representation of the situations that we find ourselves in more often than not. Sometimes, we don't even do anything to find ourselves in less than pleasant situations. But regardless of what we did or did not do to find ourselves in tricky circumstances of life, it can be extremely difficult to navigate our way through those circumstances. A lot of times, we don't even know what to do. We can end up dragging out the situation by putting it off or we can also make the situation worse by saying or doing something foolish. Life can be so hard sometimes!

Jesus says some interesting words in Matthew 7. In this moment, he is preaching a very famous sermon that is referred to as the Sermon on the Mount. After giving lots of instruction, understanding, and godly wisdom, Jesus ends his sermon by making an analogy. He says in Matthew 7:24–27:

> Therefore everyone who hears these words of mine and puts them into practice is like a wise man who built his house on the rock. The rain came down, the streams rose, and the winds blew and beat against that house; yet it did not fall, because it had its foundation on the rock. But everyone who hears these words of mine and does not put them into practice is like a foolish man who built his house on sand. The rain came down, the streams rose, and the winds blew and beat against that house, and it fell with a great crash.

There's a very interesting parallel drawn here. In the analogy, Jesus presents us with two men. These two guys have a lot in common. They both hear the Word of God, they both have the plans to build a house, they both build their houses, and they both face a storm. Notice that the foolish man was just as successful in building his house as the wise man was. Many times, we wonder why foolish people who hate God always seem to have good things consistently come their way.

For the two men in Jesus's analogy, their similarities are nearing the end when the storm comes. The storm reveals the wisdom and foolishness of these two men. Without a solid foundation, the foolish man's house cannot withstand the storm. It's worth noting that the wise man isn't immune from the storm. He sees it, he hears it, and he feels it. But since he was wise and built his house on the firm foundation, his house stands through the storm.

If building the house on a foundation allows it to stand through the storm, why wouldn't everyone build it this way? Here's the catch. Building a foundation comes with a cost. It costs money, and it costs time. The analogy is our lives are the houses. And putting Jesus's words into practice is the investment of building our lives on a solid rock. Most people don't want to make the investment to put Jesus's words into practice. They would rather just have fun and live a life free of responsibility. They want to do whatever they want without accountability. It seems like a good life for a period, but they will realize their foolishness when the storm comes. A life built with Jesus as the foundation will still have struggles but will survive nonetheless because it's built on a solid rock.

When Jesus came to earth, he taught many wonderful things that we are told to listen to and apply to our lives. As Luke is opening up his story in the book of Acts, he mentions that he has previously written about the things Jesus began to do and to teach during his time on earth (Acts 1:1). That's a simple yet profound statement. Jesus taught us to hear his words and apply them so that we can be like a wise man. But Jesus didn't only teach things, he modeled things.

Jesus' faced difficult storms during his time on earth in the same way we do. As a teenager or young adult, you have already faced many different challenging obstacles. The odds are you will face many more. But I believe that with each obstacle you face, Jesus is cheering you on because he faced the same obstacles. Learning from his example and learning how he navigated through less-than-ideal situations will help us in our journey through life.

In the following chapters, we are going to discuss some of the most common obstacles that teenagers face in life. We are going to talk about temptation, drama, peer pressure, rejection, anxiety, anger, and how to engage our unbelieving friends with the gospel. Truthfully, adults face these things too. This book is intended for teenagers but will be beneficial for all ages. It is beneficial because it is centered on the life of Jesus. His life on earth is a great example for us, and I believe that if we were to respond the way that Jesus responded to various struggles, we would see unimaginable change in our lives.

So let's take this journey together! If we know that we're going to face the same things that Jesus faced, maybe it's worth asking, "What did Jesus do?"

CHAPTER 1

Who Is Jesus?

But he continued, "You are from below; I am from above. You are of this world; I am not of this world. I told you that you would die in your sins; if you do not believe that I am he, you will indeed die in your sins."
—John 8:23–24 NIV

'll never forget when I was five years old sitting in my usual Sunday school class. Like always, I was shy as can be and ultimately didn't want to be there. In my effort to not talk to anyone, I would play with my little cell phone that my mom had given me when she bought her new phone. This was in the year 2000. Believe it or not, most kids didn't dream of having a cell phone until they were in college back then! All the other kids were fascinated that I had a cell phone at such a young age. They would ask me, "Is that a real phone?" I was so proud of my response, but I also wanted to play it cool. So I would just say, "Yes…of course it is."

I was the coolest kid in the class for a few seconds until they asked me to call somebody. It was then that I had to confess that my phone was not activated. The fascination wore off, except for with one little boy named Andrew. He was in disbelief that I had a "grown-up" phone. His fascination turned into jealousy rather quickly. Before long, he was begging me to let him play with it. In my five-year-old mind, a real grown-up cell phone was not a toy that you let other people borrow just to play with, whether it could call people or not. I don't know if I was too shy and scared to lose my toy or too selfish to share it, but I wasn't going to give up my deactivated cell phone. Andrew's jealousy turned into a temper tantrum. Pretty soon, he told the teacher that I wouldn't let him play with the phone. Andrew left out the details that this was my personal cell phone and that it was technically real. To my surprise, the teacher was on Andrew's side! She came over to me and said, "Evan, can Andrew have a turn with the cell phone?"

I then explained to the teacher that this wasn't a toy. It was my own personal cell phone. But then the teacher said, "Well, what would Jesus do?"

It was the first time I had ever heard that question before. I found it rather strange. My thought process was "Well, I didn't know that Jesus had a cell phone that his friends wanted to use." As I write this, years later, I can't help but think, why didn't she give Andrew a turn with *her* cell phone?

Since that frustrating Sunday, the phrase, "What would Jesus do?" has become one of the most popular phrases that I know. It seems like the times that the question has been raised the most is in circumstances that are similar to the one I had in Sunday school that day. It is always raised as a question of condemnation or to guilt the one that it's being asked to. But having somebody play the Jesus card every time I acted contrary to the way somebody thought I should be acting made the question lose its effectiveness. The question became so popular that I would disregard the question and the person who asked it as soon as they said those four famous words.

As a kid, the biggest drama I faced was fighting with my brothers or getting in trouble for not cleaning my room. Anytime I heard "What would Jesus do?" it was always for something minor like sharing a toy, cleaning my room, or not finishing my homework (I was homeschooled…all my school was homework). But as I grew up through the teenage years, I saw issues that would arise become more serious than those that I faced when I was a kid. Now I was facing issues of temptation and sin. There was peer pressure, drama, fear of the future. Friends would come and go. Insecurities were prevalent. At times, I had to fight thoughts of doubt, regret, bitterness, unforgiveness, and everything in between. It was facing these issues that I began to realize what real life was. Real life is hard! Thankfully, I was facing these things at a time in my life where I was really pressing into God's word. Sin seemed hard to avoid, but deep down in my soul, there was a burning desire to honor God with my life. I was reading the Bible daily and trying to learn what God's will for my life was. Yet it seemed impossible to fully devote my life to Christ with issues constantly arising.

As I was reading through the Bible, I came across two life-changing verses that I will forever cherish. The first one was John 16:33. Why this verse had never been taught to me, I could never figure out. This beautiful verse reads, "In this world you will have trouble. But take heart! I have overcome the world." As I read this verse for the first time, it seemed like a light bulb came on in my head. I didn't have to be living a perfect life with no issues to be pursuing Jesus. I could pursue him in the midst of life's messes. I mean, he gave us a warning that these messes would come. As beautiful as this verse is, I found the second one to be even more profound.

Hebrews 4:15 was the second verse. It reads, "For we do not have a high priest who is unable to empathize with our weaknesses, but we have one who has been tempted in every way, just as we are—yet he did not sin." When I realized that Jesus was with me as I faced situations that would come up, I began to deal with them in a different way. Instead of keeping my pursuit of Jesus and my messy life separate, they could be one in the same. As I have studied scripture, it is my conviction that in the one life that Jesus lived on earth, he felt every emotion that any human would ever face. As Hebrews says, he can empathize with our weakness. My mindset as a teenager started to change because I didn't have to try to figure out my issues on my own. I could turn to Jesus because he has faced the same things that I face.

It was at this point in my life, the famous question started to come back in my head when different issues presented themselves. As things came up, I stopped and thought, *Well…what* would *Jesus do?* Before the question seemed silly. But now it seemed relevant. Jesus has faced this issue before, so how would he deal with it? In my search for these answers, my prayer was that I would start reacting to my different issues the same way that Jesus did. This search did not last only in my teenage years. It's been a continuous journey to learn the heart of Jesus. Instead of asking, "What *would* Jesus do?" I think we should ask, "What *did* Jesus do?" When we ask this question, it not only helps us *learn* the heart of Jesus, but it provokes us to *live* like Jesus. The call to humanity all throughout scripture is to be holy as God is holy (Lev. 11:44; Lev. 19:2; Matt. 5:48; 1 Peter 1:16).

Who is the *Real* Jesus?

If we desire to live like Jesus, we first need to make sure we know who Jesus even is. Knowing the real Jesus is absolutely essential. Man-made religions claim to follow Jesus, yet they all have a different version of him. It is often the case that in our own lives that we too create our own version of Jesus that is not the Son of God as described in the scriptures. Paul even warns the Corinthians about this in 2 Corinthians 11:3–4. He writes:

> I am afraid that just as Eve was deceived by the serpent's cunning, your minds may somehow be led astray from your sincere and pure devotion to Christ. For if someone comes to you and preaches a Jesus other than the Jesus we preached, or if you receive a different spirit from the Spirit you received, or a different gospel from the one you accepted, you put up with it easily enough.

Did you catch that? Paul is worried for the Corinthians because he fears that their faith is so shallow that if somebody preached a different Jesus to them, they would just accept it.

Whether we have an image of Jesus who is always mad and disappointed with us or one where Jesus is just like a big loving teddy bear in the sky, we all have a tendency at times to create a Jesus of our own imagination that is not the Jesus of the scriptures. This has never been more obvious than it is these days. There are strong opinions today over how Jesus would handle the lifestyles of homosexuals. When Christians take a biblical stance on this issue, some supporters of the

LGBTQ community will appeal to the life of Jesus to point out the love and acceptance that he would have for them. They will say things like, "Jesus didn't condemn people, he would love them" or "Jesus hung out with sinners." There is *some* truth to these statements, but they don't tell the whole story. People will say these things about Jesus as if they are completely true, yet they won't even know where the story or verse comes from. They rarely quote chapter and verse when appealing to Jesus and what they end up doing is appealing to things that they've heard or made up without actually studying the scriptures for themselves. The reality is, Jesus told unbelieving Jews to their face that unless they believe that Jesus is God, they will die in their sins (John 8:24) and in verse 42 of John 8, he tells them that they are not children of God! This Jesus of scripture would be unfamiliar to many people. It's easy to create a false view of Jesus when we let our opinions and lifestyles dictate who he is instead of letting the scriptures define who he is. Christians are guilty of doing the same thing. In our effort to react to the issues that we face in the same way that Jesus would, we first need to have a solid understanding of who he is. Not who we have made him out to be, but who he *really* is.

Jesus—Fully God

You know, there's nothing like learning the story of Jesus firsthand by reading it for yourself. I grew up being taught the story of Jesus. But when I began to study the life of Jesus for myself, I found a different Jesus than the one I knew as a child. I grew up thinking that the story of Jesus began in Matthew 1:1. I now firmly believe that the story of Jesus begins in Genesis 1:1. Quick side note: If you are seeking to learn the full story of Jesus, the beginning of the Bible is a great place to start. The Bible is one cohesive story from beginning to end. Most people don't show up to the movie theaters halfway through the movie. However, if you need to learn the gist of the gospel faster, read the Gospel of John. It's only twenty-one chapters and can be read in one hour!

Back on track: As a young kid, the best image of who Jesus was, was somebody who loved me and died on the cross for my sins. This is a good image of Jesus I suppose. After all, these are the basic truths found in John 3:16. But just like anything else, as I grew up, my perspective of who Jesus was began to grow deeper. As I would read through the gospels as a teenager, I would find several instances where Jesus was controversial and a little rough around the edges. But as those areas of Jesus's life magnified, his love and compassion became more real than I had realized as a child. I had to unlearn some things about Jesus that I had developed in my mind. One of those things was how I saw Jesus in comparison to God. When we say that Jesus is the Son of God, we tend to put him a step lower than God in our minds. We may think that Jesus is really close with God or that Jesus knows him better than anyone else, but ultimately, we're lowering him to "not quite God." However, this is simply not the case. Jesus is God! You may have heard the word "Trinity" before. Lots of Christians make the Trinity a difficult concept to grasp. The truth is, it's not difficult and it's not a concept. The Trinity refers to God the Father, God the Son, and God the Holy Spirit. God is three coequal and coeternal distinct persons who share the nature and being of God. The three persons of the Trinity don't add together to equal God. Each of them is God. Not three different gods, but the one true God.

The implications of this are huge. If we're modeling our life after a version of Jesus who is a step below God or who isn't God himself, then it doesn't matter if our hearts are in the right place. We're following something that's not the true Jesus! To follow Jesus and react to life the way that he did, we have to know who Jesus really is!

A key passage in the Bible to understanding the real Jesus is found in John 1:1. It says, "In the beginning was the Word, and the Word was with God, and the Word was God." It's clear that whatever this "Word" is, it is eternal. The Word is not created but has always been in existence. This Word was also with God. Not only so, but John says that this Word *was* God! But that was in the beginning. In the present tense, we could say this Word *is* God. So what is this Word? Well, if we read a little farther, we get to John 1:14 which says, "The Word became flesh and made his dwelling among us." Aha! We now see that the Word that John was referring to in verse 1 is actually the Son of God who took on flesh (became human) and made his dwelling among us. The Word is Jesus. Now that we know this, another way to read John 1:1 could be, "In the beginning was Jesus, and Jesus was with God, and Jesus was God."

John 1:3 goes on to explain that Jesus is the creator of everything. Specifically, it says, "Through him (the Word, who we know to be Jesus) all things were made; without him nothing was made that has been made." Colossians 1:16–17 makes a similar claim of Jesus as creator when it says:

> For in him (the Son) all things were created: things in heaven and on earth, visible and invisible, whether thrones or powers or rulers or authorities; all things have been created through him and for him. He is before all things, and in him all things hold together.

Both of these verses unequivocally claim that Jesus was active in creation. And what we know from the creation account in Genesis is that it was *God* who created the heavens and the earth. Hence, Jesus is God. Colossians 2:9 elaborates more by stating, "For in Christ all the fullness of the Deity lives in bodily form."

Jesus—Fully Man

There are so many more passages that explicitly demonstrate the Deity of Jesus. To claim that Jesus is anything less than God is unfaithful to the scriptures. Yet even being fully God, he was also fully man. The fancy term for this is the "hypostatic union." It's a term used to describe the dual nature of Jesus, his divinity and humanity, as one individual existence.

It's really fascinating to think about Jesus being God. But what's more fascinating to me is that God became a man. The experiences that Jesus had as a man weren't just God pretending to have feelings or experiences. When he came to earth just as the Old Testament said he would, Jesus experienced all of the things that humans experience. He was in the womb for nine months, he was born into the world, and he had a childhood. He even got lost as a child like many of us do at some point in our lives. He grew up, he had friends, he felt joy, he felt pain, and he even did the basic requirements of a human like eat, drink, sleep, and yes, he even used the restroom. It's not farfetched to imagine Jesus sitting around a circle with his friends and laughing about a story that happened last year. It's likely that he had toothaches, stomachaches, and headaches every now and then. He probably even had the joy of catching his first fish as a child. We can speculate these things because Jesus lived a human life. In fact,

Jesus even knows what it is to die. The common things that humans experience, Jesus experienced. God took on flesh and dwelt among us. He knows what it is to be human.

Conclusion

It's comforting to know that Jesus knows what it's like to be human. But knowing that Jesus is fully God should change the way we read the Bible. It is so fascinating to read the gospels because instead of Jesus being an extremely wise guy who is really close to God, we discover that Jesus is God! This is the whole reason we are asking ourselves, "What did Jesus do?" Because Jesus is the man who is fully God but also understands what it's like to be human. You might even think of him as the God-Man. If God were a man, wouldn't you want to do the things that he did? That's who Jesus is. The God-Man.

CHAPTER 2

What Did Jesus Do Often?

**To this you were called, because Christ
suffered for you, leaving you an example,
that you should follow in his steps.**
—1 Peter 2:21 NIV

t is often said that hitting a baseball is the hardest thing
to do in sports. If you've ever been a wide receiver coming across the middle of the field, jumping as high as you
can to catch the ball, only to get your legs taken out by the
strong safety running over, all while trying to hang on to the
ball and landing on your head, you may disagree with that
statement. Or maybe you're a cheerleader who has to complete a pass where you do two flip-flops into a double-full,
only to land and do a little front punch and then be in position to get thrown in the air by your spotters and balance on
one leg several feet in the air. Okay, I guess all sports can be
quite difficult in their own way.

But consider the difficulty of hitting a baseball. Your
task is to hit a round ball with a round bat. Add that to the
fact that there is a pitcher throwing all kinds of pitches at

extremely high rates of speed. And even if you do accomplish this goal of hitting the round ball with the round bat, it still has to go in fair territory for it to count. And if you accomplish that goal, there are nine people attempting to get you out. It is no wonder why the best hitters in the world get out seven out of ten times they go up to bat.

As a high school baseball player, playing defense always came pretty natural for me. It was hitting that ultimately ended my playing career after high school. The fastest pitch I ever recall seeing in a high school game was 93 mph. All I can say is that with the tiny glimpse that I had of the ball, it looked like it was going straight in the dirt. Boy was I wrong. It ended up being straight down the middle for strike 3. Hitting and I didn't get along very well.

I never had the best batting average in high school, but that didn't keep me from trying. To give myself the best chance to hit the fast-moving pitch into fair territory without one of the nine defenders getting me out, I would observe some of my favorite professional baseball players and try to do what they did. Mechanics are everything in hitting. Without good mechanics, the odds of you getting many hits are not very good. So I would copy the mechanics and the batting stances of some of my favorite Houston Astros like Lance Berkman and Craig Biggio. After all, these are some of the best players in the world. It only makes sense to do what they would do. Granted it didn't always turn out the way I wanted to, but it still improved my batting average by imitating the pros.

If imitating a professional at their talent helps improve baseball skills or anything else for that matter, then why not try to imitate the perfect human in our journey through life? That perfect human is Jesus himself. And in fact, Paul tells us to imitate Jesus. Ephesians 5:1–2 says, "Be imitators of God, therefore, as dearly loved children and live a life of love, just as Christ loved us and gave himself up for us as a fragrant offering and sacrifice to God." It is pretty clear that Paul is confirming that the question, "What did Jesus do?" is a valid one to ask. In fact, he tells us to do the things that Jesus did.

Along the journey of life, we face countless situations. There are good times and bad times. Happy times and sad times. Times for celebration and times for mourning. Times of peace and times of confusion. There are times when we are angry, sad, scared, grieved, hurt, and bitter. When we face all of these different emotions and circumstances that life presents, it is right for us to consider how Jesus would handle the situation that we're in and try to act like that. This book is not about asking what Jesus *would* do. It's about asking what Jesus *did* do. But before we look at what Jesus did in some specific situations, we need to discuss three habits that were a part of Jesus's daily life. Essentially, before we answer the question, "What did Jesus do in *specific* situations?" we need to ask, "What did Jesus do in *many* situations?"

Jesus Spent Time in Prayer

The first habit of Jesus that we should imitate is this: Jesus spent time in prayer. When people think about Jesus and prayer, many people's first thought is the Lord's Prayer. This is a model of prayer that Jesus taught the people. It is a beautiful model of prayer that exalts the Father first. It requests that God have his way on earth just like he has his way in heaven. Jesus tells us to ask for our daily bread that will sustain us and to keep us far from anything that could stray us away from him. While this is a beautiful model for prayer, it is not the only prayer that we should pray. Reciting it from time to time is fine, but if we are imitating Jesus, the model of prayer that he gave us should be just that—a model. In the instances that Jesus would spend time in prayer, he would model the Lord's Prayer, but he would not quote it verbatim.

Jesus spent lots of time in prayer. I could even make the argument that it was the most important thing for Jesus. And why wouldn't it be? Think about it. He spent all of eternity with the Father up to his time on earth. Being in communication with the Father was very important for Jesus! But he also spent time in prayer because he relied on the power of the Father to sustain him. In fact, Jesus prayed all the time. He prayed during his baptism in Luke 3:22, he got up very early in the morning and prayed in a solitary place in Mark 1:35, and he would often pray before he would perform miracles for different reasons. Before feeding five thousand, he prayed to give thanks. Before raising Lazarus from the dead he prayed. He prayed for the little children in Mark 10:16. He prayed at the Lord's Supper. The entire chapter of John 17 is a prayer of Jesus. Perhaps his most passionate prayer is in Matthew 26 when he prayed before his arrest in the Garden of Gethsemane. One of the most amazing prayers of Jesus took place while he was hanging on the cross. Luke 23:24 records Jesus saying, "Father, forgive them, for they do not know what they are doing." Jesus prayed for forgiveness for the very people who were killing him.

The point is, prayer was an essential part of the life of Jesus. If we are striving to be imitators of Jesus, prayer needs to be essential in our lives. We cannot expect our reaction to life's craziness to be the same as Jesus if we are not living the way that Jesus lived. In fact, Paul tells us in 1 Thessalonians 5:17 to "pray without ceasing." In other words, never stop praying! The importance of prayer is certainly lost in this day and age. In scripture, prayer actually changed the outcome of things.

In 2 Kings 20, God sends the prophet Isaiah to King Hezekiah's house to inform him that he will not recover from his sickness. Isaiah relays the report that God had given him to tell Hezekiah that he will surely die. However, in 2 Kings 20:2–4, Hezekiah prays to God to heal him even though God's mind was already made up! But because of the amazing power of God, he hears Hezekiah's prayer and adds fifteen years to his life. God changes things when we pray!

Maybe this is why Paul writes in Philippians 4:6 to "be anxious for nothing, but in everything by prayer and supplication, with thanksgiving, let your requests be made known to God." If we don't pray, we are surely missing out on a special gift from God. But how can we always be praying? It may take some time to fully understand what it means to pray without ceasing. But there is something to be said for spending intentional time in prayer. So I would like to challenge you. When you wake up in the morning, kneel at your bed and spend one minute in intentional prayer. See how it affects your day. And when you go to bed, spend another minute in prayer, thanking God for allowing you to make it through the day. Maybe you'll even spend five minutes in prayer. The important thing is that you pray. It's what Jesus did. And it's what we should do. So what are you waiting for? Pray!

Jesus Loved Others

Another key habit of Jesus is that he loved other people. This one may sound obvious, but it is true. He loved others and he had compassion on people. When I was a kid, it was hard for me to comprehend why Jesus would be willing to die in my place. Now as an adult, it's still hard for me to understand it. There are times when I feel like such a failure that I question why he would give up everything for me. The simplicity of this question is John 3:16. God *so loved* the world that he sent his only begotten son. Jesus didn't come out of obligation or responsibility. He came because he so loved us. Knowing the desperate need of humanity for a savior, he came out of his love for us. Paul elaborates on this in Philippians 2:5–11 as he writes:

> In your relationships with one another, have the same mindset as Christ Jesus: Who, being in very nature God, did not consider equality with God something to be used to his own advantage; rather, he made himself nothing by taking the very nature of a servant, being made in human likeness. And being found in appearance as a man, he humbled himself by becoming obedient to death—even death on a cross!

As we learned earlier, Jesus is God. He's not one step below God. He *is* God. It takes amazing love to become a human if you're God. Yet that's exactly what Jesus did. He took on flesh and became human. Why did he do such a thing? Because he loved us.

But Jesus did not just stop there. Not only did he become human out of love for us, but he also lived a life of love during his time on earth. We must remember though, that we are in pursuit of discovering the real Jesus and not one that we make up. While Jesus did live a life of love and compassion, he certainly did not avoid controversy with others. In the life of Jesus, there is plenty of controversy, which eventually leads to his death. Yet even in this controversy, Jesus displays love. This love is on full display when he prays for those who are executing him while hanging on the cross.

To fully capture all of the instances in which Jesus showed love to people, you simply must read the gospels. While we cannot recount all of the times that Jesus demonstrated love in this book, we can highlight a few encounters that Jesus had.

You may have read through the gospels before at some point in your life. Or maybe you've read through one or two of them. If you haven't, today is a great day to start! In any case, as you study the gospels, you will find that they are filled with Jesus performing miraculous signs. Many of these miracles involve healing people. In the opening chapter of Mark's Gospel, we are told a story of a man who has leprosy. I just have to say, of all the things that I'm thankful for, not having leprosy might be on top of the list. Not only is it a terrible disease that destroys your skin, in Jesus's day, lepers were considered outcasts. It was believed by society that leprosy spread to people because of their sins. This meant that they were not allowed in the city or in public areas. They had to live like animals just to survive. It was bad enough that they suffered from this disease, but they also suffered from isolation because nobody wanted to go near a leper.

But in Mark 1:40–42, we see Jesus come face to face with a leper. He's not only coming face to face with somebody who has a horrific disease, he's also coming face to face with somebody who is thought to be nothing more than a dirty sinner who needs to be avoided at all costs. I can only imagine that Jesus grew up seeing people's reactions when lepers came near. He must have seen people scurrying away when one came walking through the city. He probably heard people hurl insults and cuss words at them. They may have even thrown stuff at the lepers. Maybe a leper even got too close to Jesus one time and his mom had to come pick him up and run away with him. Whatever the case, in Mark 1, Jesus has an encounter with a leper.

It must have taken great courage by the leper to come near Jesus and boldly state, "If you are willing, you can make me clean." Jesus replies with beautiful words as he says, "I am willing." He then proceeds to heal the man who has been an outcast for years. But Mark includes some key words that are essential to highlight. Verse 41 begins with "Filled with compassion, Jesus reached out his hand and touched the man." There are two reasons this verse should not be forgotten in the story. First, Jesus surely could have healed the man with his words. Matthew 8, Mark 7, and John 4 all include instances where Jesus healed people with his words without even seeing the people he was healing. But in the leper's case, Jesus chose to reach out and touch him. The amount of love that is demonstrated with this one action is incredible. The leper has gone his whole life believing he was unlovable and *untouchable*. And with a single action, Jesus demonstrates both. The second thing that needs to be noted in this verse is the motivation that Jesus had behind reaching out and touching him. The verse says that he was filled with compassion. While the rest of the world saw this leper with judgmental eyes, Jesus saw him with compassionate eyes.

Another instance in which Jesus demonstrated love and compassion came in one of the most difficult times of his life. In Matthew 14, Jesus learns that John the Baptist had just been beheaded in prison. The strength of friendship between Jesus and John the Baptist is not entirely clear. We do know that they at least knew each other as children because they were related. Luke 1 gives us insight that the mother of John the Baptist is a relative of Mary, Jesus's mother. Whether they were good friends as children or not, we are not sure. But surely, they at least saw each other and played games growing up from time to time. As adults, John the Baptist is the one who baptized Jesus. They certainly shared a bond at least from this event.

When John's disciples brought the news to Jesus that he had been killed, I imagine that Jesus's heart sank. In fact, he reacted as many of us do when we get bad news. He just wanted to be alone. Matthew 14:13 says, "When Jesus heard what had happened, he withdrew by boat privately to a solitary place." Have you ever received bad news that made you just want to be alone? Maybe it was a huge life event like a loved one passing away. Maybe it was just a bad day at school. You may have wanted to be alone when you and your girlfriend or boyfriend went through a breakup. To be honest, I think we've all been in a place where we just wanted to be alone for a little while. But it seems like the times when we want to be alone the most is when people want to talk the most. Of course, they mean well. Have you ever gone to your room to be alone and your mom or dad have come and knocked on your door right after you went in there? Okay, maybe that's just on movies and TV shows. But something along those lines has likely taken place in your life. I know when somebody tries to talk to me when I want to be alone, I politely tell them I am not in the mood to talk. It seems like a normal thing to do. But that is not Jesus's reaction in this situation.

The rest of Matthew 14:13 goes on to say, "Hearing of this, the crowds followed him on foot from the towns." The people in this case are kind of like your mom coming and knocking at your door when you want to be alone. The next verse says, "When Jesus landed and saw a large crowd, he had compassion on them and healed their sick." This action by Jesus is astounding! He has just received some extremely difficult news and decides that he wants to be alone. But the people come after him. Rather than telling them off and saying that he needs time, he has compassion on the people!

I remember a rather pathetic time when I wanted to be alone. It was 2010 and the Houston Texans were playing the Jacksonville Jaguars. Fifteen-year-old Evan lived for Texans games on Sunday afternoons. This game was no exception. It was a back-and-forth game, and at the end of the fourth quarter, there were three seconds left and the game was tied at 24. The Jaguars had one last chance to throw up a Hail Mary and try to win the game. As the ball was coming down in the end zone, my favorite player, Glover Quin, jumped up and hit the ball to the ground to send the game in to overtime…except that the ball didn't hit the ground. It landed in the arms of wide receiver Mike Wallace. The Jaguars won the game 30–24. I was so shocked and upset that I just ran in my room and slammed the door. About five minutes later, some of my friends came in to try to cheer me up. Rather than being receptive to their comfort, I popped off on them and yelled at them to leave me alone…over a football game.

Jesus's reaction to the people coming was certainly better than mine. And it all came from what was in his heart. Love and compassion for the people.

There is one final instance that we will highlight in which Jesus was full of love and compassion. This comes in Matthew 15. In this section, Jesus is doing ministry in full swing. Matthew 15:30–31 says:

> Great crowds came to him, bringing the
> lame, the blind, the crippled, the mute
> and many others, and laid them at his
> feet; and he healed them. The people

were amazed when they saw the mute
speaking, the crippled made well, the
lame walking and the blind seeing. And
they praised the God of Israel.

For just a second, put yourself in the mind of one of
these people. You've heard about this guy named Jesus who
has been healing people and preaching life changing sermons.
You think for a minute that you might have a chance to get
healed from whatever issue you're battling, so you make the
trip up this mountain to see this Jesus guy. You may be lame,
deaf, or blind. You may not have even been able to talk for
your entire life! And now that you've had this encounter with
Jesus, you are healed from whatever it was that you suffered
from.

Your level of gratitude would be sky-high! What more
could Jesus do after this? Have you ever helped somebody
out of a difficult situation and felt good about yourself? I
remember the first time I stopped on the side of the road and
bought somebody gas. I felt like a hero. But what did I do
after that? Did I give them extra gas money or buy them a
cold water? No. Actually, I just went home.

Jesus doesn't stop after helping the people though. He
goes the extra mile. Verse 32 says:

Jesus called his disciples to him and said,
'I have compassion for these people; they
have already been with me three days
and have nothing to eat. I do not want
to send them away hungry, or they may
collapse on the way.'

Following this statement, Jesus precedes to miraculously feed the entire crowd of four thousand men, not counting women and children. Was it not enough that he already healed people of their terrible diseases and physical handicaps? To the normal person, yes. But Jesus was filled with compassion for the people. He didn't stop halfway. He was more concerned with their well-being than just healing sick people. Again, it needs to be noted that he did not feed the people out of obligation or responsibility. He fed the people out of compassion for them.

The love and compassion of Jesus is a key aspect of his life that we should always strive to imitate. If we desire to live a life the way that Jesus lived, we must love people and have compassion on them.

Jesus Took Up His Cross

There is one final habit from Jesus's life that we will discuss that simply must be lived out if we desire to live the way that Jesus lived. This one sounds less familiar than the others but it is crucial to the life of Jesus. Jesus lived out what it means to take up your cross. We have already highlighted Philippians 2:8 in which Jesus came down from heaven and became obedient to death. But not just any death…death on a cross!

But what does it mean to take up your cross? Matthew 16:24 says, "Then Jesus told his disciples, 'If anyone would come after me, let him deny himself and take up his cross and follow me.'" This is a strange statement for a couple of reasons. First, a cross in ancient days was a well-known mechanism for death. Whereas today a person who committed a serious crime may be sentenced to several years in prison or maybe even be sentenced to death by lethal injection, in ancient days, death on a cross was the ultimate punishment. It would be strange to hear that, if we want to follow Jesus, we must take up our electric chair. But that is essentially what Jesus is saying to his listeners in the first century. Anyone who wants to follow him must die.

The second reason that this saying by Jesus is strange is because at the time he said it, he had not even died on the cross yet. Those who heard it must have been so confused. He was talking about a cross before anyone even knew that he would actually die on a cross!

So why does following Jesus require taking up our cross? A better way to say it might be, "Why does following Jesus require us dying?" The first part of Jesus's words are equally important to note. Before we take up our cross, we must deny ourselves.

It is no secret that I love sports. I love playing sports, I love talking about sports, and I love watching sports. My main teams are my Houston professional teams. The Astros will always be my favorite team, but the Texans and Rockets are not far behind! My love for professional sports is so strong that there really isn't much room for college sports to find its way in. But I still enjoy watching college football on a nice September Saturday. But since I don't really love a particular college football team like I do my pro teams, it's easy to be a fair-weather fan. I suppose I could always hold out hope that my HCU Huskies will make it big one day (please say some prayers). But until then I'll root for the University of Houston. The thing with UH is, if they're playing well, I'll cheer them on. If they're playing badly, I'll just watch another game. Because I really don't care that much. I'm really just waiting for Sunday to get there so I can watch the Texans. Oh, and go to church of course…

But when it comes to following Jesus, there is no such thing as being a fair-weather fan. It's a life commitment. You either go all in or you don't go in at all. That's why Jesus starts off Matthew 16:24 by saying a key word. *If.* If you decide to follow Jesus, you must deny yourself and take up your cross. By following Jesus, you make the decision to follow him even when life isn't so good. You don't live in a current life of sin, and you must be willing to lose anything for the sake of Jesus. Jesus even says that anyone who loves their father or mother, son or daughter, brother or sister, their spouse or even themselves more than him is not worthy of him (Matt. 10:37; Luke 14:26).

In high school, I had a guilty pleasure. Now it's a pleasure that carries no shame. That is my love for Taylor Swift music. Put me behind the wheel in a youth van on a nine-hour road trip with T-Swift jamming…Mmm, that's the life. One of her songs is about a relationship struggle with a boy. I know, that narrows it down, right? But one song in particular is called "Forever and Always." There is a lot of confusion to my girl Taylor because this boy does not seem to be committed to the relationship anymore. But once upon a time, he said he would stay forever and always. Unlike the boy in this song, a life of following Jesus means you follow him forever and always. You don't give up on God when life gets hard. You come after him harder. He comes first forever and always.

But here's the beauty of following Jesus. You have two choices. You can choose to live life your own way. You can seek to fulfil your own desires, passions, urges, surges, impulses, and everything in between. And the truth is that life can be very pleasurable…for a season. But that season doesn't last. It will ultimately cost you your life. The other option you have is to surrender your life to Jesus. Lay down your desires, your passions, your dreams, your life plan that you've figured out for yourself and choose to follow Jesus. It may cost you your life. But that's where the very next verse comes into play! The second part of Matthew 16:25 says, "Whoever loses his life for my sake will find it." If you want to see what it truly means to live, lay down your plans and follow Jesus. That is exactly what the disciples did. They left their families, their careers, and their plans because following Jesus was better.

Conclusion

It is crucial that we understand a prerequisite to living a life like Jesus means praying, loving others, and denying ourselves and taking up our crosses. But Jesus doesn't expect us to do it before he did it. As we mentioned, Jesus didn't just teach us things, he modeled them. He taught us how to pray, what it looks like to love others, and what it means to take up your cross. But he also modeled it. He prayed, he loved others, and he took up his cross. His cross was a literal cross. And losing his life meant his physical death. If we want to be like Jesus, we have to lose our life and take up our cross. Not just when life is good or when we feel like it. But every day. Forever and always.

CHAPTER 3

What Did Jesus Do with Temptation?

**Because he himself suffered when he was tempted,
he is able to help those who are being tempted.**
—Hebrews 2:18 NIV

Have you ever wondered how old you have to be to know the difference between what's right and what's wrong? If you've spent enough time around church, you've probably heard that the answer to this question is when you reach "the age of accountability." While this is not a biblical principle and it does not carry weight over the salvation of a child, it's an interesting concept. There are several different ideas, theories, and opinions on when one truly reaches the age of accountability. Basically, whenever a child begins to understand that they have options to do what is right or wrong, the age of accountability has been reached.

Reaching the age where you know right from wrong truly is different for everybody. My guess would be that most people don't remember the day that they reached that age. But believe it or not, I remember the day that I reached the age of accountability. I was only four years old. My siblings and I were homeschooled, and my older brother Erik had a friend named Taylor who lived right across the street. Since his mom was working when he got home from school, he would always come straight to our house when he got off the bus. One day he came in and he had some candy with him. Taylor was only in the second or third grade, but he was very clear with me. He said, "Evan. This is my candy. Do not eat it."

Something weird about me: I don't really care for cake, and I can definitely do without pie. But I sure do love candy. I was a fairly good kid, so I didn't bug him about his candy too much. But you see, he left it on the shelf in our living room when he left that day. Still, I knew that he would be back for it the next day, so I left it alone.

But the next day came around, and while Taylor was at school, the temptation to eat some of that candy was so strong. I mean, you can't really blame me. He has two full packets of Strawberry Sour Punch Straws. But I held off. He came home from school that day, and I asked him if I could have some. Once again, I was denied access to the heaven candy. My cousin Ana was a little bit older than Taylor, and she was in the room with us when I asked. I was expecting Taylor to remember them when he went home, but for the second day in a row, he forgot them on the shelf. I thought, *Taking one won't hurt, right?* as if he wouldn't notice that the candy was open. So when the room was empty, I opened one of the packages and I started eating one of the sour punch straws. But while I was eating it, Ana walked back in the room. She wasn't the one I was scared of at the time, but her presence sure came back to haunt me. The next day, Taylor came over and saw that his candy had been opened. He immediately went to my mom and dad and told them that I ate his candy. My mom then asked me if it was true. It was at this moment that I believe I reached the age of accountability. Because I flat denied it, knowing that I was lying. I knew it was wrong, but at least I wouldn't be in trouble. Or so I thought. There was one piece of evidence that I overlooked. Ana was in the room. And she didn't take long to throw me under the bus. She excitedly gasped and raised her voice to my mom. "I know who took the candy!"

I tried to hide my pounding heart, but I think my eyes were wider than they had ever been when I looked at her and pleaded with her not to tell on me with my stare.

Then she said, "It was Evan. I saw him take it."

Looking back on it now, shouldn't that public school girl know that snitches get stitches? I guess she wasn't scared since we were homeschooled and didn't know what that meant.

The debate of whether or not I took the candy went on for hours. At least it felt that way. In the end, my parents let me off the hook. They talked to me about how serious it was to lie. They let me get away with it, but looking back on it now, I'm pretty sure they saw right through me. It will actually be funny to see if they remember that day when they read this for the first time.

Now I understand that this is just a silly little story from my childhood. But this is exactly how temptation works. It usually starts out with a small desire to satisfy your body in some way and when the desire is acted upon, it will make you spiral out of control and will get you into messes you never thought you would find yourself in.

There is an essential aspect of temptation to keep in mind. That is, being tempted is not a sin. It's when temptation is acted upon that it becomes sin. The prerequisite to acting upon a temptation is *considering* the temptation in the first place. This happens to me every time the Astros make it to the playoffs. It starts out with the realization that the

Astros will be playing in a playoff game fifteen minutes from my house. Then a temptation to be in attendance for that playoff game sneaks its way into my mind. At first, I shake the temptation because I know that I can't afford $300 tickets. But then time goes by…and then some more time… and then I start thinking about what it would be like to be at the game. I start thinking about the excitement, being in the crowd, the views…I even think about the smell of the ballpark! Before long, the consideration of paying my life savings away becomes a possibility. And it usually ends with me pressing the "Confirm order" button on Stubhub and paying thousands of dollars to be at the game. It stings even more when they lose the games too. The fact is, if I would never consider the idea of going to a playoff game, I would still have a lot of money.

The best way to stop a temptation in its tracks is to not even move to the consideration phase. Because when you are tempted, there is more at stake than meets the eye. In Philippians 4, Paul tells us to think about things that are true, noble, right, and pure. David's prayer in Psalm 19:14 is "May these words of my mouth and this meditation of my heart be pleasing in your sight, Lord, my Rock and my Redeemer." If the things we think about and the things we mediate on are pleasing to the Lord, it will be much harder for temptation to find its way in.

When I was a four-year-old kid trying to fight off the desire to eat the candy, I never imagined that it would turn into a lie that I would have to cover up. The punishment for a lying four-year-old is maybe a time-out, grounding, or spanking if your parents are old-fashioned. But the punishments for giving into temptation when you're older get a lot more serious. They can come in the form of broken relationships, lost friendships, and sometimes even prison. That's why when we are tempted, we need to recognize it for what it is—a lie. Temptation promises satisfaction. But that satisfaction is so incredibly temporary, and the direction that your life can take as a result of it can last a lifetime.

So what are we to do? We're human. Sexual temptation is a real thing. And we're surrounded by it everywhere we turn. You may think to yourself, *How can I not look at stuff on my phone from time to time? Everybody does it.* Let me just tell you. I get it. It is hard and it doesn't make it easier knowing that everyone else is doing it too. It makes it seem like a normal thing to do. But sinning was never God's design for humanity. Giving into sin of any form does not have to be normal. I know my advice and encouragement is all fine and good, but I don't want to leave it at that. I want to get back to the point of the book. What did Jesus do?

This is where the question can start to lose its effectiveness. I know what you might be thinking. "What did Jesus do if he faced temptation? Seems like a dumb question." And I understand. Of course, Jesus didn't sin by giving into temptation. But do you remember the verse we looked at earlier? Let's look again.

> For we do not have a high priest who is
> unable to empathize with our weaknesses,
> but we have one who has been tempted
> in every way, just as we are—yet he did
> not sin. (Hebrews 4:15)

Think about it for a minute. The verse is saying that Jesus was tempted in *every* way. Not just some ways. He was tempted in the same ways that you are tempted today, but he did not sin. Is it so crazy to think that Jesus may have had sexual desire? I don't think so. After all, as we discussed, he's not 50 percent God and 50 percent human. He's fully God and fully human. Not to mention Satan knew that he was the Son of God who came down to earth to take away the sins of the world. It might not be crazy to think the target on Jesus's back was a little bigger. We know that Jesus was tempted in every way, but how did he deal with it? It turns out that the Bible talks about some of Jesus's temptations.

The First Temptation

Matthew 4 records three consecutive temptations that Jesus faced. I believe the key to unlocking the chains of temptation in our own lives can be found through the ways in which Jesus was able to overcome the temptations he faced. Let's look at some verses from Matthew 4.

> After fasting forty days and forty nights, he was hungry. The tempter came to him and said, "If you are the Son of God, tell these stones to become bread." Jesus answered, "It is written: 'Man shall not live on bread alone, but on every word that comes from the mouth of God.'"[1] (Matthew 4:2–4)

There are a few things that jump off the page from this first temptation that Jesus faced. First of all, isn't it interesting that Jesus is tempted with bread after he hadn't eaten for forty days and forty nights? This is relatable to the same temptations that we face, but it isn't always about food. The key to understanding this is that temptation seems to always be prevalent when we are weak. It may come when you've

---

[1]   Jesus is quoting Deuteronomy 8:3.

gone a while without giving into the temptation. It might also just come when an opportunity presents itself. If you want to overcome your temptation, you are going to have to remember that the devil is an opportunist. And a patient one at that. He waits patiently for the time when you are weak to offer the temptation. And that's when we tend to give in the most. I think we can agree that after going over a month without food, Jesus was weak. However, we must recognize that he was only weak physically. I don't see any evidence that would point to Jesus being weak spiritually. In fact, he's so spiritually healthy, that even when he is offered the very thing that will end his physical pain, he does not give into his bodily desire. The outer man was weak, but the inner man was strong.

Here lies an essential question for us. How healthy is our inner man? It's a question we don't ask ourselves nearly enough, but one that we should ask ourselves every morning when we wake up. Because if we are not spiritually healthy, we are more likely to give into temptation. I've never been much of a gym junky. I can't say I don't have the desire to be the most jacked 5'6" dude around. But I'm starting to accept the reality that that's probably never going to happen. Maybe this is why 1 Timothy 4:8 has always been one of my favorite verses.

> For physical training is of some value, but godliness has value for all things, holding promise for both the present life and the life to come.

I just figure, if godliness has more value than physical training, why would I torture my abs to death at the gym? Obviously, I am kidding. Being physically healthy is very important. But I think that spiritual health is often over-looked and not that important for the average person. The truth is, being spiritually strong is crucial for overcoming the evil one.

If you're anything like me, you've had numerous moments when the temptation was in your face, and like it or not, you were not strong enough spiritually to reject the temptation. I have good news for you. We are not the first people to feel this way. Paul has some things to say about temptation in his letters to the Corinthians. First:

> No temptation has overtaken you except what is common to mankind. And God is faithful; he will not let you be tempted beyond what you can bear. But when you are tempted, he will also provide a way out so that you can endure it. (1 Corinthians 10:13)

Whatever temptation you deal with, you're not alone. Other people deal with it too. And don't ever buy the lie that you have no choice but to give into temptation. There is always a way out of it. Paul goes even further in 2 Corinthians as he tells a more personal story.

> In order to keep me from becoming con-ceited, I was given a thorn in my flesh, a messenger of Satan, to torment me. Three times I pleaded with the Lord to take it away from me. But he said to me, "My grace is sufficient for you, for my power is made perfect in weakness." Therefore I will boast all the more gladly

about my weaknesses, so that Christ's power may rest on me. That is why, for Christ's sake, I delight in weaknesses, in insults, in hardships, in persecutions, in difficulties. For when I am weak, then I am strong. (2 Corinthians 12:7–10)

Bible scholars and experts can debate for days on end as to what the weakness was that Paul was referring to in this passage. And let me just say, I have a huge amount of respect for men and women who have devoted their lives to studying Paul's letters and the rest of scripture. Many of them suggest that it is highly likely that this was a physical infirmity and maybe not a temptation at all. But I think we can draw from the lesson that Paul learned regardless of what the thorn in his flesh represented. The lesson is that God's grace is sufficient for us and his power is made perfect in weakness.

This is exactly what we see in the first temptation of Jesus. In the midst of his weakness, the power of God is on full display as he boldly rejects the satisfaction that the temptation promises. The temporary, fleeting satisfaction.

The Second Temptation

The temptations didn't stop with turning stones into bread though. There were more to come. Matthew 4:5–7 says:

Then the devil took him to the holy city and had him stand on the highest point of the temple. "If you are the Son of God," he said, "throw yourself down. For it is written: 'He will command his angels

> concerning you, and they will lift you up in their hands, so that you will not strike your foot against a stone.'" Jesus answered him, "It is also written: 'Do not put the Lord your God to the test.'"

The first lesson we should learn is to not drop your guard. Rejecting a temptation is great, but there can always be another one waiting for an opening. But the most significant detail of Jesus's temptations is the way he responds to them. Did you notice that Jesus answers every temptation with a quote from scripture? It's so interesting that Satan decides to play the scripture game with Jesus. The devil now knows that Jesus knows the Bible. So he decides to quote some scriptures too. Unlike Jesus, Satan tries to manipulate the scriptures to say something that it doesn't say. The scripture that the devil quoted is a true scripture! It's from Psalm 91, and he's saying that God will protect those who trust in him. But the passage never implies that since believers have God's protection, that they should go up on a high place and jump off so that God can prove it. And Satan knows that if Jesus jumps off, that he will be committing sin by testing God. This is why Jesus is such a great example for us. He won't let the scripture be twisted. He quotes the scripture back to Satan from Deuteronomy 6:16 which says, "Do not put the Lord your God to the test."

Did you catch that? Jesus modeled for us how to stand up to temptation…but he also modeled for us how to stand up against false teaching. How does he do it? By using the scriptures. You see? Jesus knows the absolute truth because he knows what the Bible says! He was grounded in God's Word. And if we want to be able to stand up against temptation, we must be grounded in God's Word just like Jesus!

The Third Temptation

However, the temptation isn't done yet. Matthew 4:8–9 says:

> Again, the devil took him to a very high mountain and showed him all the kingdoms of the world and their splendor. "All this I will give you," he said, "if you will bow down and worship me."

You might wonder how Jesus bowing down to worship Satan could possibly be real. I mean, did Satan really think that Jesus was going to bow down and worship anyone other than God, let alone the devil? Believe it or not, this is a real temptation. Think about it. The Old Testament is chalked full of promises that the Messiah will be a King and the obedience of the nations will be his. He will have an everlasting dominion and his kingdom will reign for all eternity. Yet to become the king who will reign over the nations, Jesus has a lot of suffering to go through. He's going to have to be rejected by the people, he'll be betrayed, beaten, mocked, spit on, abandoned, denied, humiliated, tortured, and ultimately killed. That's a lot of suffering to go through. And here Satan is, offering all of the kingdoms to Jesus without any of the suffering. To be honest, this deal seems too good to pass up. It's only logical to choose the option without suffering. There's just one big problem. The logical option will force Jesus to violate God's Word. Which is why, without hesitation, Jesus replies to the devil in verse 10, saying, "Away from me, Satan! For it is written: 'Worship the Lord your God, and serve him only.'"

Time and time again, rather than relying on his own ability to reject the evil one, Jesus turned to scripture. Hebrews 4:12 says, "For the word of God is alive and active. Sharper than any double-edged sword." Of course, the New Testament had not come into form in Jesus's day, but the truth was the same. Jesus knew the power of scripture and turned to it when the devil tried to throw lies his way.

This should be a model for us as well. There are times when we can't think of any reason not give into the temptation. The opportunity is just right, we have the desire to give in, and it doesn't seem like it's going to be that bad. In fact, it may even seem logical. This is when scripture comes into play. Because it doesn't matter how small the sin is. If it is contrary to the Word of God, it is a sin. In Jesus's case, he most likely didn't have a scroll of the Torah to go look up the verses before he quoted them to Satan. Jesus was able to quote the scriptures because *he knew the scriptures*.

We already highlighted the importance of prayer in chapter 2, but how important is reading scripture in your life? Jesus knew the scriptures so well that he was able to quote them when he needed them. They were bound in his heart and imprinted on his mind. If we want to be like Jesus, we need to make Bible reading a top priority in our lives! If it's not already, it may take some time to make reading the Bible a daily habit for you. You may need to read just one chapter a day or maybe even one verse a day. Spending time reading the Bible often gets pushed aside because there always seems to be something more important that needs our attention. But let me assure you, time spent reading the Bible is time well spent. So don't wait until you're facing a situation to look up a good Bible verse. Start reading the Bible now! I love what Paul says in 2 Timothy 3:16–17 as he writes, "All Scripture is God-breathed and is useful for teaching, rebuking, correcting and training in righteousness, so that the servant of God may be thoroughly equipped for every good work."

There's a word that stands out from the above verse. That word is *useful*. All scripture is useful for us to use in different situations. So if knowing scripture is important, applying scripture is essential. This is what Jesus demonstrated during his time on earth. He knew the scriptures, and he applied them to his life.

My dad and my brothers have an unusual passion for their motorcycles. I guess it's not that unusual. Most bikers love their bikes more than life itself. I don't think their love for their bikes is at that level yet. But the three of them have joined a few different motorcycle ministries throughout the years. I know what you're thinking. Motorcycle ministry? Yes. It's a thing. And it gives them amazing opportunities to lead people to Jesus! One of the groups that they rode with for a while was called the Ambassadors for Jesus Christ Motorcycle Ministry. This group was founded by a guy who formerly rode with the Bandidos. I don't know what you know about the Bandidos, but it's pretty much the exact opposite of a motorcycle ministry group. One of my favorite parts about my family's motorcycle groups is that they have nicknames for each other. It's so funny to me to hear people call my dad *Rojo*. That's my dad's biker name. The guy who started the Ambassadors went by the nickname, *Hollywood*.

My dad and Hollywood became quite close through their conversations with each other. My dad would always talk about his amazing testimony and how he had now become one of the godliest men he knew. One random night, my dad and I were watching a game. My dad got what he thought was going to be an ordinary phone call. But this call was not so ordinary. He received news that his friend Hollywood had suddenly died in his home. The cause of death was unknown. All my dad knew was that his friend was gone.

The next few days were rough as the following days usually are after losing a loved one. My dad would talk about what a godly man Hollywood had become ever since making the switch from riding with the Bandidos. So I asked my dad what it was that made him such a godly man. I'll never forget the answer my dad gave me. He said, "His life was the application of the Bible." He explained to me that his passion for loving God and loving others was like nobody else he had ever known. I can't think of a better way to be remembered after I die one day than by being someone who was known for applying the truths of scripture to my life.

Conclusion

Taking the scriptures that you read and implementing them and applying them in your life is the key to overcoming temptations and it is the way to becoming more like Jesus. This is not just good advice; this is a command from the Bible.

> Do not merely listen to the word, and so deceive yourselves. Do what it says. Anyone who listens to the word but does not do what it says is like someone who looks at his face in a mirror and, after looking at himself, goes away and immediately forgets what he looks like. But whoever looks intently into the perfect law that gives freedom, and continues in it—not forgetting what they have

heard, but doing it—they will be blessed
in what they do. (James 1:22–25)

In your battle with temptation, remember that you are not the only one dealing with such things. Even Jesus was tempted. But he did not consider the earthly things that he would receive. He skipped the consideration phase and went straight to scripture. What will you do the next time temptation comes your way? Remember that being tempted is not a sin, and you have a chance to honor God when you are tempted. But if you start to consider the temptation, you're close to losing the fight. When tempted, run straight to scripture and apply the truths of scripture to your life. Just like Hollywood. Just like Jesus.

CHAPTER 4

What Did Jesus Do with Drama?

**In your relationships with one another,
have the same mindset as Christ Jesus.
—Philippians 2:5 NIV**

After a long day, short day, hard day, easy day, or any day for that matter, one of my favorite parts of the day comes when I turn off the lights and I have a peanut butter sandwich and a big glass of milk in my hands. I know, it sounds super weird. And eating a sandwich at the end of the day is definitely not healthy. But what makes it one of my favorite times of the day is that this is the time when I wind down and watch one of my favorite TV shows. Over the years, I've had a few different favorites. For a long time, it was the *Fresh Prince of Bel-Air*. I switched between *Friends* and a couple others for a while. But this was before I was introduced to *The Office*. *The Office* ruined other TV shows for me because no matter how great they are, they'll never be *The Office*. Now, I do admit that I also love *Parks and Recreation* and *Brooklyn 99*. But neither one of those have dethroned *The Office* as my all-time favorite.

The reason that I love these TV shows (and tend to binge-watch them) is that they allow me to escape the realities of the world for a little while. Whether this is healthy or not is a different discussion, but it works for me. The thing about all my favorite TV shows is that they don't have drama in them. Okay, honestly, they all have drama in them. But the drama is overlooked because of the comedy that they contain. Michael Scott, for example, makes a lot of decisions that cause drama, but it's a funny kind of drama.

My mom and sister, however, love watching the shows that have extreme amounts of drama. The life-changing events that happen in these shows is insane! I mean, has any hospital had more doctors get murdered, married, and divorced than *Grey's Anatomy*? Every time I find out they're watching it, I ask them how many doctors have been killed in that episode. *Grey's Anatomy* is only one of their many favorite shows. They also love *Law and Order, Breaking Bad,* and other high-suspense shows. Okay, I'll admit, *Law and Order* is pretty awesome. But those kinds of shows are all about adding as much drama and suspense as possible. Now that I think about it, real life seems to fall somewhere in between the two genres for the average person. Some people, though, always find themselves in the middle of drama, while others have the attitude of Leslie Knope from *Parks and Recreation* or Jake Peralta from *Brooklyn 99*. Some people have really great attitudes and never seem to be wrapped up in dramatic situations.

For teenagers though, it really doesn't matter how great your attitude is. If you're around other teenagers, you will find yourself wrapped up in drama at one point or another. That's just the way it is. One of the hardest parts about being a youth pastor is dealing with drama in the youth group. Not because it frustrates me. In fact, I'm more than happy to help teenagers come to a place of reconciliation after going through some drama. But it's hard being a youth pastor because drama has a way of driving others away from the church like no other. Sometimes, the drama is small, and sometimes, it's big. But when drama enters the picture, it's almost a guarantee that somebody isn't coming back to youth group. That's what's frustrating.

Sometimes, the reason friendships dissolve is harmless, and life just leads people in different directions. Other times, something happens that causes two friends to no longer be friends. One time, a junior high student bragged to me about his new girlfriend in the youth group. After reminding me about his girlfriend for a few weeks, I saw the two of them sitting together. She seemed to be annoyed, and I motioned for her to come talk to me. I asked, "Are the two of you dating?"

She was so embarrassed and humiliated by the thought. She quickly exclaimed, "No!"

I said, "It's okay if you are."

She did not relent. She adamantly replied, "We're not! We never were, he just tells people that!"

I then assured her that I would handle it. I told the junior high boy to stop telling people that, and I broke the news to him that she does not want to be his girlfriend and he needs to leave her alone.

That was a rather easy (and pretty funny) dramatic situation to solve. Other times, it's more difficult. The loss of friendship hurts. You've probably lost a friend or two at some point and I know I have certainly lost some friends through the years. In fact, it really is just part of life. But losing friendships due to drama is what hurts the most. And I can't act like I'm completely innocent when it comes to causing drama.

Truthfully, I caused a lot of it in high school. In ninth grade, I started dating this girl named Haley. Two of her friends and two of my friends were dating each other, and the four of them were all keeping their relationships a secret from their parents. So I figured that I could date Haley and keep that a secret too. But Haley had different ideas, and since I wasn't on board with that, our relationship lasted two and a half days. That wasn't the end though. As high school went on, Haley dated a couple of guys, and I realized I had missed my chance to be with her. I told myself if I ever had a chance to get back with her that I would take it. The opportunity did indeed present itself the summer before we started our senior year. The problem with that is, I had been talking to another girl at the time. But I wasn't gonna miss out on Haley again. So I went for it this time. The drama that resulted from that decision in our friend group was more than I ever thought possible. And to be honest, it never really got resolved. Maybe that's because Haley and I are still together and are married now. I don't have any regrets about making my move on Haley. But I definitely could have handled the whole situation in a wiser way that could have resulted in less drama.

Drama is a tough word to put an exact definition on. For the sake of this book, we will focus on some of the drama that teenagers face. But even then, it would be wrong of me to say that drama happens one way every time. Drama can be crazy, messy, confusing, unique, and hurtful in many different situations. But I think the majority of the time, drama among teenagers happens in one of two ways. The first is when people talk about you behind your back, and the second is when loved ones turn their back on you. The good news for us, in our journey to be like Jesus, is that Jesus faced both of these kinds of drama in his life! A closer look at them will help us navigate the drama that comes up in our lives.

Getting Talked About

Jesus spent a lot of time teaching different crowds of people. If you want to learn more about Jesus's teachings, give Matthew a read. It is full of the teachings of Jesus. And as Jesus would teach, people would often gossip about him after he was done. This was typically done by the Pharisees, Sadducees, High Priests, and other experts of the law. And this sort of thing happens in Matthew 15. Read these verses:

> Jesus called the crowd to him and said, "Listen and understand. What goes into someone's mouth does not defile them, but what comes out of their mouth, that is what defiles them." Then the disciples came to him and asked, "Do you know that the Pharisees were offended when they heard this?" He replied, "Every plant that my heavenly Father has not planted will be pulled up by the roots. Leave them; they are blind guides. If the blind lead the blind, both will fall into a pit." (Matthew 15:10–14)

As Jesus is teaching the people, it seems like the disciples are aware of something that Jesus may not know. That is that the Pharisees are offended by his teaching. Did the disciples hear them talking about Jesus afterward? Did they bring their complaints to the disciples? Whatever the case, the disciples come to Jesus to alert him that he has offended the Pharisees and that they are now talking about Jesus behind his back.

Have you ever had a moment where people you weren't even that close to talk behind your back? It happens to all of us at some point. A lot of times, it might even happen on social media. The culture that we live in says that we can't let someone disrespect us. It says that we have to stick up for ourselves because if we don't nobody else will. There's often a temptation to confront the person or the people who are talking about you and tell them why they are in the wrong. The problem with this is that when this happens, we don't just tell them they're wrong. We fight back. And when we fight back, things can get ugly real fast.

Isn't it shocking then, how Jesus responds when he hears that the Pharisees are talking about him? Wouldn't you expect Jesus to ask his disciples which ones said something? That's our response. "Who said that? I'll go get him right now." But that's not what Jesus does. Jesus basically tells his disciples to not worry about the Pharisees. He says that they are blind guides. In other words, Jesus says, "The Pharisees will get theirs in the end, so why do I need to worry about them?" And here is a great lesson for all of us when people talk about us behind our backs. Let God handle it. They will get theirs in the end, but there is no need to justify yourself or even to defend yourself. Just leave them alone. Paul even writes in Romans 12:19, "Do not take revenge, my dear friends, but leave room for God's wrath, for it is written: 'It is mine to avenge; I will repay,' says the Lord."

When it comes to this form of drama, not doing anything seems doable. But what about when a close friend is the one that causes drama? Well, believe it or not, Jesus faced that too.

Stabbed in the Back

Many people would say that the ultimate betrayal in the history of the universe has to be when Judas betrayed Jesus and turned him over to be killed. Judas was one of

Jesus's twelve disciples and lived life with Jesus for quite some time. He saw Jesus teach people, heal people, love people, feed people, and even bring dead people back to life. And this is the same guy that would turn Jesus in to be arrested and ultimately killed. But on the other hand, we're not told much about Jesus and Judas having a super close friendship. At least not on the level that Jesus was friends with Peter, James, and John. It certainly seems that these three are Jesus's best friends. Obviously, it would hurt worse if one of them betrayed Jesus. Well, it may not go down as a betrayal, but the ultimate stabbing in the back that Jesus felt was not from Judas. It was from his best friend, Peter.

There were actually multiple times when Peter assured Jesus that he would not let him get hurt. In Matthew 16, Jesus was telling his disciples about the things that had to happen to him. He explained that he had to be handed over to chief priests and suffer many things and eventually be crucified. As Peter heard these words, he was appalled. Verse 16 says, "Peter took him aside and began to rebuke him. 'Never, Lord!' he said. 'This shall never happen to you!'" Peter receives a pretty strong rebuke for this, but this passage encapsulates Peter's determination to protect Jesus.

Even after Jesus predicted that Peter would disown him in Matthew 26, Peter says in verse 35, "Even if I have to die with you, I will never disown you." This is a bold statement by Peter. He tells Jesus that his love for him is so deep that he will go to the point of death with him. This is a deep friendship. Do you have a friend that loves you so much that they would be willing to die with you? It's hard to know for sure since we're not really put in those situations. But I'm willing to bet that you have someone or you have had someone in the past whom you consider to be a best friend. What makes having a best friend so great is that you always have somebody who you can trust and who will be with you in tough times.

I remember a time playing baseball in my junior year of high school when my teammates made sure to have my back. I was the catcher, and a runner was coming home from third. As soon as I caught the ball that came from the outfield, I turned to tag the runner out. But to my surprise, this runner was not sliding like most runners do. He was coming in headfirst like a linebacker sacking a quarterback. I'm already a generally small guy and this guy was… well, let's just say he was not a small guy. And when you add the fact that I was in a defenseless position, you can imagine that this collision didn't end pretty for me. I got hit and did a complete backflip and a half before landing on my back. How that happens, I have no idea. I was very disoriented after landing, and I looked in my glove and was surprised to see that I held on to the ball. After I realized I was alive and had successfully tagged the runner out, I looked up at the runner, and my third basemen Joey was already on top of this guy. My pitcher Kyle was right behind Joey with the rest of the team on their way as fast as they could. There was a little brawl, multiple ejections, and I had a concussion. But I learned something that day. My teammates were more than just my teammates. They were my brothers. It was not okay that somebody would try to hurt me.

It's comforting having somebody you can trust to have your back. I imagine that Peter thought he would be like my third basemen who would be ready to risk it all to come to Jesus's defense. Peter even told Jesus that he would be willing to die with him. But when the lights were on Peter and it came time for him to put his money where his mouth was,

Peter fails. The scene is recorded in Matthew 26:69–75. The drama is too good not to read, so here it is:

> Now Peter was sitting out in the courtyard, and a servant girl came to him. "You also were with Jesus of Galilee," she said.
>
> But he denied it before them all. "I don't know what you're talking about," he said.
>
> Then he went out to the gateway, where another servant girl saw him and said to the people there, "This fellow was with Jesus of Nazareth."
>
> He denied it again, with an oath: "I don't know the man!"
>
> After a little while, those standing there went up to Peter and said, "Surely you are one of them; your accent gives you away."
>
> Then he began to call down curses, and he swore to them, "I don't know the man!"
>
> Immediately a rooster crowed. Then Peter remembered the word Jesus had spoken: "Before the rooster crows, you will disown me three times." And he went outside and wept bitterly.

Peter had good intentions to stick with Jesus through it all, but when Jesus was being arrested, Peter left him all alone. Let's talk about Jesus's perspective on this for a second. He's arrested in the middle of the night. He's being beaten, spit on, and mocked. Oh, and one more thing—he's alone. We've already mentioned that Jesus was fully human, and just like any human would be, Jesus was scared. There is nothing that Peter could have done to get Jesus out of this situation, but one thing that could make it more bearable would be for Peter to go through it with him. But instead of Peter being willing to die with Jesus, he decides that living is the better option.

I love the way that the *Passion of the Christ* movie portrays this scene. Peter denies Jesus for the third time, and Jesus just looks at Peter. He doesn't beg Peter to tell the truth. He doesn't yell at Peter. He doesn't say, "I told you so!" He doesn't even talk bad about Peter. He just does nothing. As we mentioned earlier, when people that Jesus was not close to talked about him behind his back, Jesus did nothing. And when Jesus's best friend Peter stabs him in the back, Jesus still doesn't do anything. I believe that the reason Jesus doesn't do anything is because he knows better than anybody that his actions or desires will not be able to control somebody else. Nobody made Peter deny Jesus. He did that on his own. And rather than trying to convince Peter to not abandon him, Jesus lets the betrayal happen.

Betrayal causes a pain that is unlike others because a bond of trust that has been built up over time is broken. You have likely experienced this in your life. It may not look identical to the betrayal that Jesus felt, but most of us have had friends turn their backs on us a time or two. How do you handle it when this happens? Most of the time, we gossip about them to other people, send them a nasty text, or block them on social media. But I think the most appropriate response if we want to be like Jesus would be to do…nothing.

I'm sure doing nothing when a friend stabs you in the back is not the advice you typically receive, and it's certainly not what we want to do. But it's what Jesus did. So the next time you feel that you've been betrayed, try doing what Jesus did and just do nothing. But don't stop at that, because that's not the whole story!

Seeking Reconciliation

You see, Jesus didn't do anything initially. But he definitely did something that is hard for all of us to do. He offered forgiveness. The whole concept of forgiveness is counter to the culture that we live in today. The culture that we live in today says, "If they walk out of my life, I'm locking the door behind them." But you see, when people walked out of Jesus's life, he left the door open for them. When Jesus was hanging on the cross and dying, he actually prayed for those who were executing him. In Luke 23:34, Jesus proclaims from the cross, "Father, forgive them, for they do not know what they are doing."

Call me crazy, but it is my belief that the Father listened to Jesus and forgave those who hung him there. When Jesus asked for forgiveness for the sins of those men, I don't think he was being sarcastic. I think Jesus was dying for the forgiveness of them just as much as the forgiveness of you and me.

But what about his best friend Peter? Did Jesus have a chance to forgive him? Well, he didn't have a chance to tell Peter he forgave him before he died on the cross, but he sure did after he rose from the dead. In John 21, we are given a window into the reconciliation that takes place between Jesus and Peter. John 21:18–19 says:

> "Very truly I tell you, when you were
> younger you dressed yourself and went
> where you wanted; but when you are
> old you will stretch out your hands, and

someone else will dress you and lead
you where you do not want to go." Jesus
said this to indicate the kind of death by
which Peter would glorify God. Then he
said to him, "Follow me!"

I think there are two things that need to be highlighted
here. First, Jesus's words to Peter seem harsh. How is it that
by telling Peter how he is going to die, that Jesus is offering
reconciliation? Well, Peter missed his chance to die with Jesus
the first time. And as crazy as it sounds, Jesus is giving Peter
another chance to die. It won't be with Jesus, but it will be for
Jesus. This is exactly what ends up taking place. Numerous
ancient writings describe that after many years, Peter died by
being executed the same way Jesus was. Except Peter requested
that his cross be put in the ground upside-down, because he
did not feel worthy enough to die the way that Jesus died.

But there's one more brilliant part of Jesus's forgiveness
to Peter. This is when he said the words, "Follow me!" Once
upon a time, Peter was nothing but a fisherman making a
living on a boat. That all changed in Matthew 4 when Jesus
looked at Peter and said the words, "Follow me." When Peter
heard those beautiful words for the second time, I can only
imagine that memories came flooding back in of the first
time he heard those words. By saying "Follow me" again,
Jesus wiped the slate clean, and Peter knew that he had been
forgiven for the wrong that he had done to Jesus.

Think about the people who have wronged you. Has
the door been locked behind them? I'm not saying to go out
and chase them and beg them to come back inside. But do
they know that you are ready to offer forgiveness? What better way is there to be like Jesus than to see reconciliation take
place with someone who has wronged you?

When we consider how much we've already been for-given ourselves, forgiving others should come naturally. Our sin against God deserves the punishment of death. As you may already know, the wages of sin are death, but the gift of God is eternal life in Christ Jesus our Lord (Romans 6:23). In light of the forgiveness we've received time and time again, our response to others who wrong us should be to forgive them. Jesus tells us in Matthew 6 and 18 that, unless we forgive others when they sin against us, we should not expect to be forgiven. And guess what? When you recognize the incredible debt that you've been forgiven, it makes forgiving others a joyful thing!

I already mentioned that growing up, my siblings and I were homeschooled. There was another homeschool family who we were best friends with. This family was the Fletcher's. We spent a lot of time at the Fletchers' house, and they spent a lot of time at our house. There were a few things that were iconic about the Fletchers' house. They had a blue fif-teen-passenger van that we called the Fletcher-Mobile, they always had amazing sweet tea, and they had a ditch behind their house that we would play in all the time. But one of the most iconic things about the Fletchers' house that I remem-ber was the really long table they had in their dining room. Mary and Kenny Fletcher had eight kids, numerous grand-kids, and their kids' friends go to their house a lot, so a big table was essential. In my nine-year-old mind, this table had to be forty or fifty feet long and there was always a spot for someone else to sit. I could never imagine that table running out of spots.

I like to think of being a Christian as having a seat at Jesus's table. And at Jesus's table, there is a seat for everyone. So that begs the question, who has a seat at your table? Are there some people who have lost their seat at your table? The problem is, when people start losing their spots at your table, it doesn't just hurt them. It also hurts you. When there is no reconciliation for the wrong that has taken place, your life is a breeding ground for bitterness to grow.

Bitterness is a very dangerous thing to play with. As you probably know, on September 11, 2001, the terrorist group Al-Qaeda flew airplanes into the World Trade Center Towers in New York City. They thought that flying the planes into these towers would knock them over. However, the towers stood their ground. This was not the end of the story though. After several minutes went by, the towers eventually collapsed on top of themselves. The impact of the airplanes did not cause them to fall immediately. However, the impact of the planes did cause fire to spread up and down the entire building. When the fire consumed the buildings, they collapsed.

When friends do something to hurt you, it can be like the initial impact of the airplane. It hurts, but it doesn't destroy you. But if you let the impact of the offense consume you, it will ruin your life just like the fires consumed the buildings and destroyed them.

Conclusion

The next time somebody causes drama in your life, remember what Jesus did. He didn't do anything to seek revenge. He knew that he couldn't control somebody else's actions. But he also didn't let the offense cause bitterness. He was always ready to offer forgiveness and seek reconciliation. Peter didn't lose his seat at Jesus's table, and neither have you. I'll ask again, is there anybody who has lost their seat at your table? I challenge you to make your life like a big table. A big table like the Fletchers' and, more importantly, like Jesus.

CHAPTER 5

What Did Jesus Do with Peer Pressure?

Therefore, since we are surrounded by such a great cloud of witnesses, let us throw off everything that hinders and the sin that so easily entangles. And let us run with perseverance the race marked out for us, fixing our eyes on Jesus, the pioneer and perfecter of faith. For the joy set before him he endured the cross, scorning its shame, and sat down at the right hand of the throne of God. Consider him who endured such opposition from sinners, so that you will not grow weary and lose heart.
—Hebrews 12:1–3 NIV

If you do a simple Google search on the world's population broken down by country, you will find that the USA has almost 5 percent of the world's population. You will also quickly find that despite only having 5 percent of the world's population, we have a staggering 25 percent of the world's incarcerated prisoners right here in the United States. Now, before you go critiquing my research, I know that these numbers are not exactly accurate. They fluctuate with time, and there are some discrepancies when you factor in third world countries with fewer laws and countries in Asia who may not have accurate reporting. However, even if the numbers are slightly less than 25 percent, the numbers are still rather shocking. Let me also say, that I am not writing this to make a political statement. The only reason I bring it up is to say this: in the United States of America, a lot of people go to jail.

As a teenager approaching adulthood or even as an adult, we must realize something—we are all one dumb decision away from prison. There are of course a number of different ways to find yourself in prison. Obviously, causing physical harm to another person can land you one of the longest sentences, especially if you kill that person. Many adults can find themselves behind bars because they found ways to start embezzling money from their jobs. What seems like a flawless plan often turns into a disastrous nightmare when questions start being raised about the funds they were handling. Then of course,, there is always robbery, kidnapping, and extortion. I suppose we should also mention that not paying traffic tickets, excessive speeding, and gambling can be other nonviolent ways to end up in jail. But I think some of the quickest ways for a normal person to wind up behind bars are to get mixed up with drugs, alcohol, or sexual immorality.

My dad has been a licensed professional counselor for the majority of his adult life. He's had great success as an LPC and helped countless people through life's challenges. He even served as the chair for the state capitol representing all Texas LPCs for several years. My point is, he's seen a lot. He has obviously never broken confidentiality by talking to us about one of his clients, but one thing he has always told us is that he's never heard any of his clients say that they were glad they tried cigarettes, drugs, or alcohol for the first time.

He also tells us he's never had anyone say they were glad they saw pornography for the first time. These are some of the things that lead to people going to jail for DUI's, possession, sexual assault, and child pornography. Yet every inmate who is serving time for one of these crimes has one thing in common. They all had a first time. They had a first sip, a first hit, a first smoke, or a first glance.

If we could ask some of the people who are in jail for crimes related to such things now, I'm sure it is safe to say they wish they had never tried it for the first time. So why did they try it for the first time? I think it's the same reason many of you reading may have tried some of these things for the first time: peer pressure.

When I think of peer pressure taking place, I have an image where five friends are standing in a circle and four of the friends are staring at one and putting the pressure on him or her to take the first smoke or take the first sip. While that may happen from time to time, that is definitely not the way peer pressure takes place most of the time. A lot of times, peer pressure happens without anyone even offering anything. Other people's actions can cause you to feel pressure from them without them ever asking you to do anything. If your friends all seem to be having sex with their boyfriends and girlfriends, you may feel or have already felt the pressure to also have sex. The same is true of drinking, smoking, vaping, masturbating, and endless other sexual acts. There are certainly smaller forms of peer pressure as well. Cussing, posting inappropriate stuff on social media, and even finding a boyfriend or girlfriend can all be caused by pressure from your peers.

Whether it was a small thing or a major thing, I'm sure you can recall a time when you felt some form of peer pressure. The truth is, you probably continue to feel forms of peer pressure just based on our society today. You may be asking yourself how it's possible that we can learn from Jesus on this issue. Jesus never had peer pressure to smoke, drink, post certain things, or cuss. There is no record that Jesus had peer pressure to view any form of pornography either. So how can we learn from what Jesus did if he never faced the issues of peer pressure that we face today?

Well, Jesus may not have felt peer pressure to smoke or drink, but there are several instances where Jesus is put in situations where peer pressure is taking place. Even though it may involve different specifics, we can still learn from Jesus's example on what he did with peer pressure.

Jesus as a Child

Nearly all the records of Jesus in the New Testament are in reference to his adult life. We're told a few details about his birth, but even those do not compare to the amount of literature that is written about the events of Jesus as an adult. The details of Jesus's life that we have in scripture are completely sufficient for everything we need to know and believe that Jesus is the Messiah. But we do have one event from Jesus's childhood in the New Testament that I think is worth highlighting. This takes place in Luke 2.

Rather than reading the whole passage, I'll give you the gist of the situation. Every year, Jesus would travel with his family to Jerusalem for the Festival of the Passover. One year, when Jesus was only twelve years old, they made their annual trip. After the festival was over, the whole traveling party left town and began their journey back home. There was just one problem: Jesus wasn't with them. It took his parents a whole day to even notice he was not in their company before they began freaking out and panicking. If you've never heard this story, it turns out that Jesus stayed behind in Jerusalem, listening to teachers and asking them questions. This certainly seems like an odd thing for a twelve-year-old boy to do. Anytime my daughter isn't ready to leave somewhere, the easiest way to get her to come is to simply say, "Okay, bye, Zoe! I'll see you later." The thought of being left behind motivates most kids to drop what they're doing and go where they are supposed to go. But that's not the case with Jesus. It appears from this passage that he is no ordinary child. The reason I bring up this story is to point out one thing. That is, Jesus did not just go with the flow. He was different. The peer pressure that many of us face is to just go with the flow of what everyone else is doing. When everyone is on Snapchat, you feel a pressure to also be on snapchat. When TikTok is the new thing, we go with the flow and get a TikTok. But Jesus was not concerned with what others were doing. Now, was it wise to stay behind and cause his parents anxiety? Probably not. Even though he never sinned, Jesus still had to learn what the wise thing to do was. Luke 2:52 says that Jesus *grew in wisdom.*

Obviously, that's just a minor example of how Jesus didn't cave to what others expected of him. But it's important because in his adult life, we see many other situations where Jesus is put in very serious predicaments. But now, he is fully grown in wisdom. And the way he handles peer pressure as an adult will certainly give us better insight into how we can respond to peer pressure.

Jesus as an Adult

Getting into a debate can be the worst. Especially if it's about politics! To be honest, I get in political debates sometimes. I tend to get in even more arguments when it comes to sports. I will defend my 2017 World Series Champion Astros until the day I die! But the problem with little arguments or debates is that rather than ever getting somebody to see your point of view, they just get more entrenched in their point of view. The same is true of you as well. The truth is people have different opinions. Sometimes, we cannot understand how people could possibly have an opinion that's different from ours when we feel strongly that we are right, but that's how opinions work. They're different!

Even though we already know that we are unlikely to convince somebody to change their opinion, it usually does not stop a debate from taking place. One thing I have found when I have been in friendly and unfriendly debates is that people will ask me hypothetical questions. They ask these questions because they know that I will be forced to give an answer that they believe will fit their agenda. The truth is, this is a form of peer pressure, and it is something that Jesus faced on more than one occasion.

One instance where Jesus felt this form of peer pressure comes from Mark 12. I consider this to be a pretty savage moment that Jesus had. Honestly, it's too good not to read.

> Later they sent some of the Pharisees and Herodians to Jesus to catch him in his words. They came to him and said, "Teacher, we know that you are a man of integrity. You aren't swayed by others, because you pay no attention to who they are; but you teach the way of God in accordance with the truth. Is it right to pay the imperial tax to Caesar or not? Should we pay or shouldn't we?" But Jesus knew their hypocrisy. "Why are you trying to trap me?" he asked. "Bring me a denarius and let me look at it." They brought the coin, and he asked them, "Whose image is

this? And whose inscription?" "Caesar's,"
they replied. Then Jesus said to them,
"Give back to Caesar what is Caesar's and
to God what is God's." And they were
amazed at him. (Mark 12:13–17)

While it may seem like a weird answer that Jesus gave
to the Pharisees and Herodians, it is rather fascinating! They
had given Jesus two options. If Jesus were to answer with
either of these options, things would have gone bad. If Jesus
said that they should pay their taxes, then he would have lost
all of his credibility with the people. The tax rate was insanely
high and unfair. Anyone who was for paying taxes would be
against the good of the common people. On the other hand,
if Jesus would have sided with not paying taxes, he would
have certainly been arrested on the spot with a rightful conviction. So this is a lose-lose situation for Jesus. But he's on
the spot. He has to give an answer under extreme pressure.

But Jesus doesn't give in! He knows that the people truly
do have an obligation to pay their taxes because they enjoy
the benefits of things that the government provides. But at
the same time, he knows that the government leaders also
need to give God what's his. Their worship, their devotion,
and ultimately their lives.

I find it interesting that Jesus was asked a question that
had nothing to do with God, yet his response had everything
to do with God. Maybe this can be a lesson for us. How
often, when we're asked a question, do we consider the way
that God sees it? To truly know the heart of God though, we
must spend time with God! This will help you in any form of
peer pressure you find yourself in.

As awesome as this encounter was, I think the encounter
that Jesus has in John 8 tops this one. In John 8, Jesus was

doing his thing and teaching people. This was almost always to the displeasure of Pharisees and teachers of the law. In this particular case, the Pharisees decided to step up their game. Rather than just asking Jesus a difficult question about the Old Testament law in an effort to prove their point, they actually brought a real-life person before Jesus—a person who has been caught breaking the Old Testament law. The particular offense was that they brought a woman who had just been caught committing adultery. Leviticus 20:10 makes it clear that if somebody is caught in this act, they are to be put to death. The peer pressure that Jesus was facing in this moment was much more than a difficult hypothetical question. They were putting Jesus in a position where he would have to decide the fate of woman who was clearly guilty. The dilemma that he was facing was serious: if he lets her off the hook, they would have a basis to charge Jesus with breaking a law. At the same time, if he has her killed to be in accordance with the law, then Jesus isn't a whole lot different than the Pharisees.

There is a tremendous amount of hypocrisy taking place here by the Pharisees. They're demanding that the Old Testament law, which is good, be acted upon to bring about justice. Yet they are ignoring that King David, whom the Pharisees hold in high esteem, was also guilty of adultery and deserving of death when he slept with a woman named Bathsheba in 2 Samuel 11. The only reason he didn't die for his sin is because 2 Samuel 12:13 says that God took away his sin. Exodus 33:19 and Romans 9:15 both say that God will have mercy on whom he has mercy. Therefore, if God sees it fit to show mercy and forgive someone of their sin, he is justified in doing so because Jesus ultimately would pay the price for those sins through his death on the cross. Yet rather than desiring the mercy of God for the woman who was caught in adultery (which they probably set up as a trap), the Pharisees are seeking justice and wrath. For God to enact justice against sin is perfectly good and right. But the Pharisees are seeking death for the woman and not paying attention to their own sins!

Even though they are being hypocritical, Jesus is still put in a tough situation. Yet he handles this dilemma beautifully. Rather than speaking, he bends down and writes with his finger on the ground. Verse 7 says, "When they kept on questioning him, he straightened up and said to them, 'Let any one of you who is without sin be the first to throw a stone at her.'" He then bent down and wrote in the ground again. As he did this, all the people began to leave. Verses 10 and 11 say, "Jesus straightened up and asked her, 'Woman, where are they? Has no one condemned you?' 'No one, sir,' she said. 'Then neither do I condemn you,' Jesus declared. 'Go now and leave your life of sin.'"

I wish I could tell you the magic words that Jesus wrote in the ground. My dad may be on to something when he says Jesus was writing other sins in the ground that the people watching had surely committed. That certainly sounds probable. But the truth is, we don't know, because we're not told. But even with the lack of information, I think that there is a great lesson that we can learn from this story as it pertains to peer pressure. That is, you are allowed to act with love and have convictions at the same time.

It may not be true of every circumstance, but a lot of times we give in to peer pressure because we don't want to make the other people feel weird for doing something that you do not believe in. This could be the classic case of being offered a drink. It may go against your convictions, but everyone else is doing it, and you don't want to appear rude to the person offering the drink. Maybe your friends aren't going to pray before a meal and so you just go with the flow and don't pray even though it's what you normally would do. Or maybe it's the classic case that we always hear about where you're just in a group of people and somebody starts talking bad about somebody else you all know. While it may be uncomfortable, we have to realize that we have permission to refuse to join in any sinful behavior.

Standing alone with our convictions does not mean that we can't love at the same time. Notice how Jesus handles these situations. He certainly acted with love toward the woman who was caught in adultery, but he also did not pop off on those who brought the woman. Yet he stood firm on his convictions. What I'm saying is this, when you stand firm on what you believe, that does not mean that you are not acting in love. Refusing to participate in sin is always the number one priority for God's children.

Will you lose friends if you do this? Will you become less popular? Oh, don't get me wrong, those are certainly possibilities. But let's look at Paul's words in Galatians 1:10 when he says, "Am I now trying to win the approval of human beings, or of God? Or am I trying to please people? If I were still trying to please people, I would not be a servant of Christ." So what is actually more important in life? To please people and disobey God or please God and not give in to peer pressure? It is clear that pleasing God should always be our top priority.

I remember in 2020, the world was in a crazy place. We had COVID-19 going on as well as riots and protests taking place to support the Black Lives Matter movement. Also, Taylor Swift had just released a new album and I miss the old Taylor, but that's neither here nor there. When the Major League Baseball season resumed, there was a lot of talk among players on who would kneel during the national anthem as a form of peaceful protest and who wouldn't. Some teams decided to kneel before the anthem as a means of protest and then stand during the anthem. Many famous athletes who made comments about refusing to kneel have faced tremendous backlash. Perhaps none more than former Saints quarterback Drew Brees. Even Brees, however, has kneeled in the past with his teammates before or after the national anthem. The hate that Drew Brees experienced across all social media sites and news networks made it clear that there was tremendous peer pressure for every athlete to be willing to kneel as a means of peaceful protest.

But what if an athlete believed that it was wrong to kneel for such a protest? What would this athlete do when all of his or her teammates and opponents are all putting the pressure on for him or her to kneel? Well, that is exactly what happened with one San Francisco Giants pitcher. Sam Coonrod was surrounded by his twenty-nine other teammates, numerous coaches and trainers, as well as the entire Los Angeles Dodgers team all kneeling in protest. Not one person stood…except for Sam Coonrod.

Is there something inherently sinful or wrong about kneeling for such a cause? To be honest, I'm not entirely sure. But my point in writing this is not to promote or to bash the kneeling and peaceful protests that were taking place. My point in writing this is to highlight the reason that this pitcher decided to stand. When asked why he refused to kneel, Coonrod said, "I'm a Christian, so I just believe that I can't kneel before anything besides God." I applaud Coonrod for being willing to stand alone. He acted with love as he supported his teammates and opponents, but he did not bend on his convictions that he cannot kneel for any reason to anyone or anything besides God.

In the Old Testament, there is a story in the book of Daniel of three young men who also wouldn't bow to anyone besides God. This is the story of Shadrach, Meshach, and Abednego and the fiery furnace. You may have heard this story before. In the book of Acts, we see the apostles facing a very similar situation. In their case, as well as Shadrach, Meshach, and Abednego, it was a lot more like persecution rather than peer pressure, but there was still a great deal of pressure they were under. In Acts 5, Peter and other apostles were brought before the Sanhedrin to be questioned by the high priest. And it turns out, this high priest is very upset with them for continuing to talk about Jesus after they were given strict orders not to. But look at what their response was in Acts 5:29, "Peter and the other apostles replied: 'We must obey God rather than human beings!'" Wow. What if pleasing God rather than human beings was at the forefront or our minds every time we faced peer pressure?

Peer pressure is a serious thing. If you knew when it was coming, you would certainly be more prepared to stand up against it. But a lot of times, it takes place when you're least expecting it, from people who are your best friends. Whether it is to not talk about Jesus, drink, smoke, have any form of sex outside or marriage, cuss, stay out too late, gossip, or even watch a movie or TV show that you believe is wrong, pleasing people is never worth it if it displeases God.

Allow me to highlight a couple of Bible verses for your encouragement. To get the most out of these scriptures, make sure to read the whole passage they come from in their context.

> Therefore put on the full armor of God,
> so that when the day of evil comes, you

may be able *to stand your ground*, and after you have done everything, *to stand.* (Ephesians 6:13)

Resist him, *standing firm* in the faith, because you know that the family of believers throughout the world is undergoing the same kind of sufferings. (1 Peter 5:9)

Whatever happens, conduct yourselves in a manner worthy of the gospel of Christ. Then, whether I come and see you or only hear about you in my absence, I will know that you *stand firm* in the one Spirit, striving together as one for the faith of the gospel. (Philippians 1:27)

Conclusion

The next time you find yourself in a position where you are feeling pressure to give in to what everyone else is doing, stop and remember Jesus's example. He stood firm when the pressure was on, and he modeled for us how to love others and have convictions at the same time. Consider Sam Coonrod, who had already seen the reputation of his peers destroyed but was willing to stand anyway. Whatever the case, whatever the situation, or whatever the peer pressure, always be willing to take stand. And when nobody stands, stand on your own.

CHAPTER 6

What Did Jesus Do with Rejection?

**Jesus is the stone you builders rejected,
which has become the cornerstone.**

—Acts 4:11 NIV

mentioned earlier that when I played high school baseball, I looked up to Craig Biggio. There are two reasons I looked up to Craig. For starters, I'm the biggest Astros fan in the history of the universe. The second reason is that Craig Biggio is probably the most famous Astro of all time. If you were to look up a list of Astros legends, you will certainly see names like Nolan Ryan, Jeff Bagwell, and Jose Cruz. But none of these players will top Craig Biggio. Biggio is one of the only players in professional sports to play his entire twenty-year career with one team. During his time as an Astro, he made seven All-Star games, won five Silver Slugger awards, and four Gold Glove awards. He also became the first player in major league history to have at least 3,000 hits, 600 doubles, 400 stolen bases, and 250 home runs. In addition to these accomplishments, he also led the Astros to become the

National League Champions in 2005. His greatest accomplishment, however, was being inducted into the National Baseball Hall of Fame in 2015.

It's hard to imagine that the Astros could ever have a player better than Biggio…that is, until Jose Altuve came along. This is certainly a debated topic among Astros fans, but up to this point in his career, Altuve is on track to surpass nearly all of Biggio's accolades. During his entire twenty-year career, Biggio only reached 200 hits in one season. Altuve broke Biggio's single-season hits record in just his fourth year, the same year in which he became the only player in Astros history to win a batting title. In fact, Altuve recorded 200 hits or more in four consecutive seasons from 2014 to 2017. In thirteen years of playing so far, Altuve is already an eight-time All-Star and has over 2,000 hits. He has also led the Astros to four World Series in 2017, 2019, 2021, and 2022. The Astros won the World Series in 2017 in year that Jose Altuve was named the American League Most Valuable Player. He then led them to another World Series victory in 2022.

As I am writing this, Altuve has not yet done enough to have a better career than Biggio. But up to this point in their playing careers, Altuve has proven to be the better player. So what is the point of me telling you this? Well, it turns out that Jose Altuve, a man who is among the best players in Astros history and very well may be the best when it is all said and done, was originally rejected by the Houston Astros.

You see, Altuve is from Venezuela. It was there that he found his love and passion for baseball. When he was only sixteen years old, he heard about a special camp the Astros were holding where several of their scouts would be in attendance. He jumped at the opportunity and attended the camp. After the first day of camp, the scouts told Altuve thank you for coming, but there was no need to return the next day.

You see, even though he was pretty good at baseball, Altuve was only 5'6". To the scouts, it seemed like a waste of time to have Jose out for another day of camp if they already knew in their minds that he was too short to play professional baseball. To Altuve, it was clear what was going on. He had been rejected.

Rejection is one of the hardest things to face in life and even more so as a teenager. It takes place when you are completely dismissed by someone else because they do not see the value that you bring. When you are rejected, you feel invaluable, unlikeable, and unwanted. This feeling is so hurtful that we will do anything we can to avoid it. A lot of times in life, we even give in to peer pressure, simply to avoid being rejected. Humans have a natural desire to be liked, wanted, valued, and appreciated. If rejection is a possibility, we'll often do our best to protect ourselves from it.

The problem, though, is that rejection happens all the time. As you're reading this, you can probably recall a time or two when you have been rejected. I know I certainly have. I remember standing in the outfield with all my teammates and opponents while they were announcing the All-Stars when I was twelve years old. Many of my teammates' names were called, but not mine. I also remember making the All-Star team the next season only to sit on the bench nearly every game. When I finally got to play that summer, I made one error, and the coach took me out of the game in the middle of the inning, which was totally humiliating.

I also remember the first time a girl broke up with me. Even though I didn't even like her that much, the feeling of rejection still hurt. I remember times when I wasn't invited to do certain things with friends, and I remember being told I didn't get a certain job. Rejection is such a painful yet common part of our society. What are we to do?

You know the answer by now. We ask ourselves, "What did Jesus do with rejection?" Well, it turns out that Jesus faced some pretty intense rejection. The reason that he was crucified is because the people rejected him as the King of the Jews. If the rejection that Jesus faced was serious enough to get him killed, then I think we can learn a thing or two from Jesus when it comes to rejection.

Being crucified was not the first record that we have of Jesus being rejected. There are actually multiple places in the gospels where we see Jesus being rejected. Let's look at some of those.

Hometown Rejection

In Mark 6, Jesus wanted to go to his hometown to teach in the Synagogue and perform miracles for the people. And that's exactly what he was doing. Mark 6 says that many who heard him were amazed! If they were amazed, shouldn't they have had a good reaction? Verses 2 and 3 actually indicate that they had a skeptical reaction as they say:

> 'Where did this man get these things?'
> they asked. 'What's this wisdom that has
> been given him? What are these remark-
> able miracles he is performing? Isn't this
> the carpenter? Isn't this Mary's son and
> the brother of James, Joseph, Judas and
> Simon? Aren't his sisters here with us?'
> And they took offense at him.

Have you even been to a magic show or seen an illusionist? Some of the things they are able to do make absolutely no sense. I'll never forget seeing Jared Hall, a Christian illusionist, come to HBU my senior year and mesmerizing the entire student body. Including myself! But what I have found when somebody does a magic trick is that people typically have one of two reactions. They are either amazed and entertained by the illusion and they are content with being fooled or they cannot stand to see the illusion and not be able to make sense out of it. In their attempt to understand, they get frustrated and lose out on the joy of the illusion. To be fair, I am almost always the kind of guy who gets frustrated and annoyed when I am stumped by a magic trick.

Even though Jesus wasn't doing magic, I get the sense that this is the kind of reaction the crowd had. They could not accept the fact that a man they had known their whole life could have so much wisdom. So rather than being embraced by his hometown, Jesus was rejected by his people…which included his own family! Look at what the next verses say:

> Jesus said to them, "A prophet is not without honor except in his own town, among his relatives and in his own home." He could not do any miracles there, except lay his hands on a few sick people and heal them. He was amazed at their lack of faith.

It certainly seems that the rejection Jesus faced was at the very least troublesome for him. But even in his disappointment, Jesus recognizes that he is not the first person to ever experience rejection. He recounts Old Testament prophets who were commonly not welcome in their hometowns either. Much like the situation with drama, doing nothing seems to be Jesus's reaction. However, notice that Jesus still does a few miracles. Maybe he healed the people who did have faith? Maybe there were some so sick that they couldn't communicate? Whatever the case, there is something clear from this passage. Jesus didn't stop doing miracles completely. In fact, he would later continue to do miracles in other towns. Why is that? I think it's because despite the rejection that Jesus faced, he didn't let it affect his value.

A lot of times, this is where we miss the mark. When we are rejected, we believe that the rejecters are right. It's so easy to believe that the rejecter's opinion of us is the correct opinion and so we lessen the value of our talents, passions, gifts, and worst of all, ourselves. Have you ever tried out for something only to find out you didn't make it? Deep down, you know that it's not personal. But the feeling of being rejected cuts deeper than not being good enough at a particular sport or instrument. The rejection makes you believe that *you're* not good enough.

Feeling like you're not good enough is the devil's playground. Because once you believe that you're the problem and that you're the one who's not good enough, you feel like you're a failure. This unlocks the door for the enemy to start whispering lies to you that can be more convincing than you ever thought possible. But just because something failed doesn't mean that you're a failure. And that's what we have to recognize.

I remember taking my first college class ever when I was a junior in high school taking dual credit classes. The first major exam I ever had was in US History 1301. I studied for the test as best as I knew how. I took the exam, and I didn't feel too great about it. When the professor gave me my grade back, my stomach turned upside down. I earned a 52. To make it worse, my professor wrote a note that said, "Not good." I certainly earned the failing grade. But the comment from my professor felt like he was rejecting the notion that I had what it takes to make it in college. Then things got worse. He wrote on the dry-erase board that the highest grade in the class was a 94 and the lowest grade in the class was a 52. I drove home from school that day as an eleventh grade boy crying in my car because I bought a lie. I bought a lie that my failure on a test made me a failure. I figured that since I failed a test and got the worst grade in the class, then I might be too dumb for college. I started trying to figure out what else I could do in life that wouldn't involve college. I let the lies that the enemy was whispering affect my value as a person.

It's easy to believe these lies. If your girlfriend or boyfriend breaks up with you, you might feel unlovable. If you get fired from a job, you might feel like a failure. If you get left out of your friends' weekend plans, you might feel like you're easily forgettable. This is where it is crucial for us to be rooted and grounded in God's love. Because even though we may feel rejection in different areas of life, if we are rooted and grounded in Christ, then we will know our value despite somebody else's rejection.

This is certainly the attitude that Jesus had in his earthly life. Remember that Jesus prayed often while he was on earth. Praying helped maintain his strong connection with the Father. And even though Jesus was rejected by people, he cared more about what his Father thought about him. Jesus said in John 6:38, "For I have come down from heaven not to do my will but to do the will of him who sent me." Through different rejections, Jesus kept his focus on doing the will of the one who sent him. What's mind-boggling to me is that Jesus is the creator of the universe and that he came to earth as a human and allowed himself to face rejection by his own creation!

The Rejected Stone

In Mark 12, Jesus tells a parable about a man who planted a vineyard. The man rented it out to farmers. Understand this, the farmers did not own the vineyard. They were only renting it. The owner sent some of his slaves to get some of the produce, but the farmers beat them to death. So the man who owned the vineyard decided to send his own son. Yet they even went as far as to kill his beloved son. Jesus said this parable and then applied it to himself by quoting from Psalm 118:22–23 which says:

> The stone the builders rejected has
> become the cornerstone; the Lord has
> done this, and it is marvelous in our eyes.

Quoting this passage to Jewish leaders was done on purpose. They knew the passage and they didn't want to believe that it was referring to Jesus. Jesus points out that they will reject him as an ordinary man who is stirring up trouble, but he will end up being the only way to the Father. He is not just any stone. He's the cornerstone. The cornerstone is laid first, and it determines where every other stone will be laid. In explaining this parable, Jesus is pointing out that he is the cornerstone whom they are rejecting. Isn't it crazy that the creator of the universe will feel the rejection of his own creation?

It hurts to be rejected. But Jesus didn't let the rejection he faced define his value. He knew his value even when others didn't. That's the lesson that we can learn from Jesus. The truth is, you are an individual who is made in the image of God. What an honor! God could have made you an ant, a moose, or a shark, but he chose to make you a human. If you are an image bearer of God, then your life has value! Don't ever let anyone's rejection of you define your value. As Jesus says in Matthew 10:29–31:

> Are not two sparrows sold for a penny? Yet not one of them will fall to the ground outside your Father's care. And even the very hairs of your head are all numbered. So don't be afraid; you are worth more than many sparrows.

Sometimes, it's hard to see our worth when other people don't see it in us. It's highly likely that Jose Altuve struggled to see his worth when the Astros scouts told him not to come back the next day. But one person who knew Altuve's worth was his dad. His dad told him to return to the camp the next day even though he was already rejected. When he showed up, one of the scouts said, "Well, since you're here already, you might as well work out with us."

As he worked out on the field that day, the scouts started to change their minds about him. They ended up offering him a very small amount of money to play at their lowest level of the farm system.

That's all Altuve needed. He excelled so fast through the minor leagues that before he ever played a game in AAA, he was called straight up to the Astros. The rest is history. It's not hard to see why Altuve was able to return to camp the day after he was rejected. Altuve is a devoted follower of Jesus. He never misses an opportunity to give God glory. When the coaches and scouts rejected him, he knew his value. Not because of his baseball ability, but because of who he is in Christ.

Conclusion

The truth is you might fail at some things in life. But just because you fail at some things doesn't make you a failure. It just means you failed at *that* thing. I failed an exam in US History, but that didn't make me a failure. I picked myself up, learned where I went wrong, and studied harder the next time. I ended up earning a B in that class. I then made it my entire undergraduate career without ever earning anything lower than a B and I graduated summa cum laude from Houston Baptist University. I didn't stop there. I ended up earning a master's degree from Liberty University. If I would have believed the lie that I was a failure after failing that test and feeling the sense of rejection from my professor, I wouldn't be writing this book today.

Whenever your identity and self-worth are rooted and grounded in what the Creator of the universe thinks of you, the opinions of others won't affect you. You'll learn to care more about what God thinks of you than man. One of the greatest Astros of all time faced rejection, and the Creator of the universe faced rejection. You can take it to the bank that you will also face rejection in this life. When you do, remember that you're already accepted and chosen by Jesus. And if you have Jesus, you have everything you need!

CHAPTER 7

What Did Jesus Do with Anxiety?

Cast all your anxiety on him because he cares for you.
—1 Peter 5:7 NIV

One of the most frustrating things in the world that most people cannot comprehend or accept is a difference in opinion. Think about it, people get in the most heated arguments (mainly on social media) about differences in opinion. When it comes to politics, Democrats can't fathom how Republicans could possibly support Donald Trump. Republicans can't fathom how Democrats could possibly support the Black Lives Matter organization. Republicans and Democrats are all people and they have different opinions. Fans of other teams don't understand how I can be an Astros fan after the sign-stealing scandal in 2017. I don't understand how they can't look at the facts and see how the Astros were wronged by MLB in the whole situation. People who use iPhones can't understand how anyone could use another phone with those ugly green text messages and lack of FaceTime ability. The few iPhone haters out there think iPhones are overrated.

The point is, with everything in life, everyone has an opinion, and they are rarely the same as other people's opinions. It's kind of like cars. When you drive down the freeway, there are hundreds of cars, but it's hard to find two that are exactly the same. There are cars, trucks, SUVs, sports cars, motorcycles, 18-wheelers, and buses. Then you factor in different models, features, colors, and you realize that cars come in all different shapes and sizes. Why are we talking about cars and opinions? Because anxiety is another thing in life that everyone has and it comes in all shapes and sizes.

I'm willing to bet that a lot of people reading this book looked at the table of contents and came straight to this chapter to find out how to get some advice for the anxiety that they're feeling. We all feel anxiety on some level. Finishing up a big assignment before the deadline causes anxiety. Fearing that your boyfriend or girlfriend might break up with you causes anxiety. When life is busy and you have a thousand things to do and only a couple of days to do it, you feel anxious. I even get anxiety when one of my teams is in a close game and it's coming down to the wire.

Of course, there are heavier forms of anxiety as well. If your loved one gets a bad doctor's report, you will certainly be flooded with fear. Struggling to pay bills is a really hard thing to deal with that causes unease. When you see red and blue headlights behind you and you realize that you are being pulled over, you get anxious about the encounter you're about to have with the police officer. The anxiety that you're feeling right now as you read this may be extremely unique and hard to put into a specific category, but it's anxiety nonetheless.

Many of the things we've already talked about like drama and peer pressure can certainly cause anxiety. And having anxiety is probably one of the worst feelings in the world. Some of the hardest days of my life took place when my brother was accused of a crime and arrested. We were able to post bond quickly, but that was only the beginning of the journey. Over the next year and a half, there were monthly trips to the courthouse for the judge to review the evidence with the attorneys. Every trip was nerve-racking, because we never knew if somebody else was going to come forward with fallacious evidence. Every month, the prosecuting attorney would tell the judge the same thing: "We're still looking for evidence." And then, the court date would be reset the next month. This meant we would have to wait yet another month and be anxious about the whole scenario, not knowing what the future would hold. For over a year, I would cry and plead with God for a favorable result because the thought of my brother being sent to prison was too much for me to handle. This was deep, deep anxiety. I even spoke with his attorney, and he personally told me that in thirty years of practicing law, he's never seen a case last this long without evidence and that this is the most ridiculous accusation he's ever heard. I then asked him, "That's a good thing, right? Doesn't that mean he'll be found innocent since there's no evidence of a crime?"

He told me, "Not exactly. The accuser is relentless, so it's not that simple."

I lost a lot of sleep and a lot of weight that year. It was hard to eat and hard to fall asleep at night knowing this uncertain future was weighing over my head. Looking back at that time, I'm so thankful for the faithfulness of God. The fear of walking into a courtroom with a judge who sends people to prison every day was a truly terrifying experience. Yet even in the valley, God was with us.

In those days, after I was finally able to fall asleep at night, the anxiety was so bad that it was physically hard to get out of bed. Literally! I felt like I had a hundred-pound weight on my chest, and it was hard to roll over out of bed. When I finally did, the day-to-day tasks of life were hard to get through. I'm sure you've had days like that too.

I've noticed that whenever we feel like this, it's hard to find energy and motivation to pray. And if we do pray, it's probably something quick like, "Lord, please take this away." That was my prayer many nights. The interesting thing is, I don't think that's the worst thing in the world! You see, even Jesus felt anxiety during his life on earth. When he had anxiety, he actually prayed that same prayer to the Father. In Matthew 26:39, he said, "My Father, if it is possible, may this cup be taken from me." In other words, Jesus was praying that he wouldn't have to suffer the things he was about to suffer.

So you may be thinking, *If my natural response in prayer when I'm feeling anxiety is the same thing that Jesus prayed, then I'm good, right?* Well, we often pray for the thing we're dealing with to be taken from us. But that's not all that Jesus prayed. Let's look at his story a little closer.

More Earnest Prayer

When Jesus prayed for the cup to be taken from him, it was during the last night of his life before he was going to die. Jesus knew that he was about to be arrested, he was going to be tortured, beaten, mocked, spit on, and ultimately crucified on a cross, hanging naked and in shame. If you knew that you were going to have people come to your house, arrest you and kill you the next day in front of a huge crowd, I think you would be a little anxious too. We have reasons to feel anxiety from time to time, but Jesus had the ultimate reason to feel anxiety!

In Luke's account of the story, he says, "And being in anguish, he prayed more earnestly, and his sweat was like drops of blood falling to the ground" (Luke 22:44). After reading that, you may think that Luke was exaggerating, because people don't sweat blood. However, there is an actual medical condition called hematohidrosis. If you do a basic Google search of the word, you find that it says, "Hematohidrosis is a condition in which capillary blood vessels that feed the sweat glands rupture, causing them to exude blood; it occurs under conditions of extreme physical or emotional stress." How would Luke know about hematohidrosis? Paul mentions Luke by name in Colossians 4:14 and calls him the doctor. Some translations say *physician.* So it actually makes sense that Luke would include the medical condition that Jesus was suffering from, because he knew what it was!

Now that we've established that Jesus sweating blood is a real medical condition caused by anxiety, let's think about how many times we've sweat blood. Or how many times do you know somebody else who has sweat blood? My guess would be zero. That tells us that the stress that Jesus was feeling was more intense than the stress that you or I have ever felt. In a weird way, that's sort of comforting. It's comforting to know that Jesus knows what we're feeling when we have anxiety!

It's easy to let the blood that Jesus is sweating dominate the passage that Luke wrote. But there's a part of Luke's sentence that we can't look over. It says that while he was in anguish, he prayed *more earnestly.* When we talk about the question, *What did Jesus do?,* this is the kind of stuff that we can't miss. Yes, you and I may say a quick prayer for God to take away the anxiety that we're feeling. Jesus prayed that too.

But he didn't just say a quick prayer. It says that he prayed more earnestly! So in the time that Jesus was feeling the most stress in his life, he also pressed into prayer! When I'm feeling heavy anxiety, I'll usually just pray the quick prayer for God to take it away and then I'll lay there feeling sorry for myself. The example that Jesus has given us is that we need to press into prayer during these times and pray more earnestly than usual!

In fact, this is the same advice Paul gives us in Philippians 4:6. He says, "Do not be anxious about anything, but in every situation, by prayer and petition, with thanksgiving, present your requests to God." The reality of life is that we don't have to feel anxiety. God even tells us not to be anxious for *anything*! All we have to do is pray in every situation.

Jesus makes a great point in Matthew 6:27 when he says, "Can any one of you by worrying add a single hour to your life?" The fact of the matter is, worrying is not required. In fact, God tells us not to do it. Believe me, I know that's hard, and sometimes, it feels like it's out of our control. Rather than seeing it as a command by God to not worry, just look at it as permission from God to not worry. Isn't that amazing? You have permission from the eternal God, who is the creator of the universe, to not feel anxious about your current situation!

Not as I Will

Before we move on to the next chapter, there is one more critical piece of Jesus's prayer that we have to learn. You see, Jesus didn't just ask for the cup to be taken from him. He also said, "Yet not as I will, but as you will." Those are some of the hardest words to pray sometimes. They're hard to pray because we know what we want. We want our will to be done. But when we pray for God's will to be done, there's a chance that his will isn't the same as ours! And that was certainly the case for Jesus. But Jesus modeled for us that the Father's plan will always be better than our own. We see things in a very temporal way. God sees them in an eternal way. He sees the bigger picture. What we think we want may not be what we need in the long run. God is not limited in time like we are limited. He sees the bigger picture, and he has the eternal perspective. If we really trust God, then we should always want his will to be done over our own will, even if it means that we have to suffer temporarily. At the same time, don't assume that God's will is definitely different than yours. His will may very well be that you would cry out to him and that he would hear you and answer your prayer to receive glory for himself. So pray earnestly!

Jesus was extremely anxious in the moments leading up to his arrest. But he didn't stay anxious. He prayed for the Father's will to be done and he knew that he was gonna have to walk the gruesome road to Calvary that would ultimately end his life. Rather than continuing to worry about it, Jesus faced it, knowing that he came from heaven to earth for this very purpose. Through public arrest, being spit on, slapped, abandoned, beaten, flogged, mocked, and ultimately killed, Jesus endured the humiliating death. Hebrews 12:2–3 says:

> For the joy set before him he endured the cross, scorning its shame, and sat down at the right hand of the throne of God. Consider him who endured such opposition from sinners, so that you will not grow weary and lose heart.

Jesus certainly felt the anxiety that you and I feel from time to time. But he also saw the bigger picture. And because he saw the bigger picture, he was willing to face what was in front of him. Not having anxiety doesn't mean that you won't feel pain in this life. It just means that you trust God's ultimate plan and you know that it's all going to work out for your good and for his glory. And if the really hard thing that you're going to face is going to work out for your good in the end, then why worry about it? It's not going to add a single hour to your life!

The God who Provides

Jesus tells us in Matthew 6:26, "Look at the birds of the air; they do not sow or reap or store away in barns, and yet your heavenly Father feeds them. Are you not much more valuable than they?" Birds don't have the awareness to plan for the future. They don't have a savings account full of worms that they can lean back on if times get tough. They don't know how they're gonna get their next meal. But they also don't worry about it. It's not in their capacity to do so because even though they don't realize it, our heavenly Father feeds them. He's the one who provides their next meal, and let me just tell you in case you didn't realize, there are a lot of birds! But one thing about birds is that they are not image bearers of God. Humans are! And that's why Jesus tells us that we are much more valuable than birds! And if he provides for the birds, you better believe that he's gonna provide for people.

When Adam and Eve were embarrassed by their nakedness, God provided clothing. When Abraham was told to sacrifice his son, God provided a better offering instead. When Joseph was sold into slavery, God elevated him to a place of authority, and he ended up saving his family. When Moses and the Israelites were stuck between the Red Sea and the rapidly approaching Egyptian army, God parted the waters so they could walk through. When they were hungry, God provided manna for them to eat. When they grew tired of eating the manna, God provided quail. When Ruth gave up her chance at having a family and carrying on her family name, God provided a husband. When Goliath was intimidating the Israelites, God provided the young warrior, David, to defeat him. When Elijah was hiding in a ravine, God provided ravens to bring him food. When Nebuchadnezzar was troubled by his dreams and was about to have all of the Jewish people killed, God provided Daniel with the interpretation of the dream. And when an entire world was dead in their sins, God provided his Son to die in our place.

God has a long history of being faithful to provide. Listen, I know the anxiety you feel is real! I know the fear of the unknown is scary. I know that it can be hard to get out of bed some days. But never buy the lie that you're in this thing alone! God has not brought you this far to abandon you now. He's the one who began a good work in you, and he is going to see it through. There is great joy ahead! The anxiety that you're facing is a great opportunity for your trust in the Lord to grow.

There's a famous story about cows and buffalo that I find fascinating. Out in the plains where wild buffalo and cows reside, there can be some major storms that swoop in. The interesting thing is that the cows can sense the storm coming, and in an effort to preserve themselves and stay out of the storm, they run away as fast as they can. Much like the cows, the buffalo can also sense the storm coming. However, their reaction is exactly the opposite. Instead of running away from the storm, they run toward it! Now that seems like a silly thing to do.

What's crazy, though, is that as a result of these two reactions, the cows end up being in the storm twice as long as they would be had they just stayed still, while the buffalo weather the storm in half the time that they would if they didn't move! What's my point? There are going to be things in life that cause anxiety. And when we face these things, it can be tempting to do things to numb the pain so that we don't feel anxious. But that's not going to make the situation end, it's just gonna prolong it.

Conclusion

The model that we have from Jesus is that even in his deepest anxiety, he trusted the Father's plan. And once he was spiritually prepared, he faced the storm head on. Whatever you're facing right now, follow Jesus's example. He prayed and he faced what he had to face, knowing that the pain was temporary, and the joy is eternal. I know the anxiety is real. I know it's heavy and I know it hurts. Remember that you have permission to not feel anxious right now. You can find comfort knowing that even the birds of the air are taken care of, and you are more valuable than many birds!

So right now, the choice is yours. You can choose to keep numbing the pain and avoiding the anxiety, or you can face it head on just like the buffalo, and just like Jesus, while remembering that you have permission from God to not feel anxious about the outcome.

CHAPTER 8

What Did Jesus Do with Anger?

**My dear brothers and sisters, take note of this:
Everyone should be quick to listen, slow to speak and
slow to become angry, because human anger does
not produce the righteousness that God desires.**
—James 1:19–20 NIV

If you've ever gone to a new school, new church, moved to a new house, or visited a new vacation spot, you probably remember having a certain image in your head about what that new place was gonna be like. When I made the All-Star team when I was thirteen years old, I envisioned our first game being in a stadium just like the Little League World Series on TV. I thought they would announce our names, sing the national anthem, have F-18s do a flyover, and basically treat us like superstars. Boy was I wrong. Our first All-Star game was anything but that. We played on the exact same field that we had played on all year, we didn't get matching uniforms, there were about nine fans watching, and I didn't even play in the game. The image I had in my head was way off.

I've noticed that what I imagine things to be like before they happen are usually far off from reality. I had thoughts about what it would be like to have a house, be married, and even have kids. Now that those things are realities, I can look back and realize that my imagination of what they would be like was completely different than what they're really like.

As we've already discussed, we have a tendency to do the same thing with our perception of Jesus. The truth is, we have no excuse for imagining Jesus to be something he's not. We have a written record that is sufficient for us to know the true Jesus of scripture. We must learn to let scripture define who Jesus is and not our imagination or what the culture might believe. Many people imagine Jesus to be a big loving teddy bear who never gets annoyed, mad, or irritated. This is simply not true. Jesus is fully human and as a human, Jesus experienced all of these emotions during his time on earth.

It can be hard to comprehend this, because we tend to associate these emotions with sin and the unequivocal claim of scripture is that Jesus is without sin.

> God made *him who had no sin* to be sin for us, so that in him we might become the righteousness of God. (1 Corinthians 5:21)

> For we do not have a high priest who is unable to empathize with our weaknesses, but we have one who has been tempted in every way, just as we are—*yet he did not sin*. (Hebrews 4:15)

> *He committed no sin*, and no deceit was
> found in his mouth. (1 Peter 2:22)

> But you know that he appeared so that he
> might take away our sins. *And in him is
> no sin*. (1 John 3:5)

To say that Jesus may have sinned a time or two based on stories in the gospels would be completely unfaithful to the scriptures and let's face it, it would be an insane and moronic claim. However, there are clear passages of scripture where Jesus is angry. How can this be?

Our experience with anger is what makes this topic cloudy. When we're angry, we tend to act impulsively and do whatever it takes to get revenge. I have so many stories about being angry on the baseball field that I could write a whole book about it. But I've also been angry over things that involved real life. When I was twenty-three, our very first childhood dog was sick. We rescued him when I was about twelve years old, and we loved this dog. However, we knew that his time would be coming to an end soon, and one day, my parents came home and found that he had died. It was sad, but not completely random. Three years later, when I was twenty-six, the unthinkable happened. I started piecing some things together about the death of my dog, and I learned that he didn't die of natural causes. He was murdered. A "friend" at the time, attempting to do the family a favor, decided to take matters into his own hands, and he killed my dog. Imagine the anger that flooded my soul when I confirmed this was true. Yes, he was sick, and yes, he was going to die soon. But that should be my family's decision to put him down, not someone else's! The amount of anger I had toward this person was almost unbearable. I immediately started thinking about what can be done for justice to be served. However, this person has essentially been out of our lives since the crime, and there's no proof of foul play.

What you'll notice from this story is that I had a legitimate reason to be angry over this situation. You may even be a little angry for me as you read this. Yet the anger that I felt didn't have anything to do with sin on my part. In this particular case, I'm free of sin. So anger in and of itself is not sin. However, anger can cause a great temptation to commit sin, and I certainly felt some of that. Most of the time when we experience this level of anger, I would say we do sin in some way. This means that even though we can be angry over a situation that we did nothing to cause, we have the opportunity to honor God when we're angry by not sinning. How can we do this when we're really angry though? A better question might be, what did Jesus do with anger? The cool thing about this question is that Jesus faced anger more than once, yet he did not sin. What a perfect person to learn from when we face anger!

Jesus at the Temple

All four Gospels record an event where Jesus entered the temple courts, and he saw people selling doves, cattle, and other things that were necessary to make sacrifices. What was supposed to be a place where people could encounter God had become a place where the rich were getting richer by charging people lots of money in order to have the chance to make their sacrifices. The result of this is people are being robbed of their money and peace with God because of the greediness of the rich. It's wrong enough to price-gouge people in general, but it's even worse when you're using God's temple to do it.

It's no surprise that when Jesus sees this, he's mad. He's so mad that John 2:15 says, "He made a whip out of cords, and drove all from the temple courts, both sheep and cattle; he scattered the coins of the money changers and overturned their tables." Wow. At face value, it sure looks like Jesus sinned. I mean, driving out with a whip? Overturning tables? How are these things not sinful? Let's take a closer look.

One of the main reasons why we sin when we're angry is because we act on our first impulse. We don't think, we just act. The classic example is giving somebody the middle finger after they cut you off in traffic. But as we look at the anger that Jesus had, we see that he did not act impulsively. For starters, we should recognize that Jesus went to the temple at the time of the Jewish Passover. This was a yearly event where people gather from all around to encounter God and remember the Israelites' departure from Egyptian captivity. There is good reason to believe that Jesus had attended this event multiple times growing up. If this is the case, then Jesus wasn't shocked when he saw what was going on. He actually already knew it would be happening and was patient. In his wisdom, he waited for the right time to take action.

However, even if he was a little shocked when he saw the scams and the price-gouging, he still didn't act impulsively. The verse says that he made a whip out of cords. He didn't just grab the closest thing he could find and start swinging. He actually took the time to form a whip. In other words, the action that Jesus was about to take was calculated, not impulsive. He only used the whip to drive out the cattle and the sheep, because that's how you make them move. It wasn't harsh, cruel, or pain-inflicting.

As he was doing these things, Matthew 21:13 records Jesus saying, "It is written," he said to them, "'My house will be called a house of prayer,' but you are making it 'a den of robbers.'" The words that we absolutely cannot overlook from this verse are, "It is written." You see, Jesus isn't just calling the robbery that he sees taking place bad because he thinks so. He actually calls it bad because God's Word says so. When he says, "It is written," Jesus is quoting Isaiah 56:7, which talks about the temple being a house of prayer, and Jeremiah 7:11 which says they have turned his house into a den of robbers. Jesus's anger is rooted in biblical truth, and by turning over the tables, he is certainly getting their attention and proving that what they are doing is sinful because it violates God's Word.

When we're angry about something, how often do we stop and think about if we are justified in our anger according to God's Word? I would say most of the time we're just mad because something didn't go our way. Jesus was certainly angry, but he didn't sin. Instead, he pointed out the sin that was taking place. This brings up a really interesting question for us to think about. Do we get angry for the things that offend God the same way that we get angry for the things that offend us?

The truth is, we tend to get angrier when we're wronged. Crazy enough, Jesus was wronged too. He was actually so wronged that he was given the death penalty for a crime he didn't commit. Now talk about a reason to be angry! Jesus should surely be mad about being murdered, right? We've already highlighted this in chapters 2 and 4, but it's amazing that in this moment, Jesus says in Luke 23:34, "Father, forgive them, for they do not know what they are doing." Stop right there. Try to understand what you just read. While Jesus was hanging on the cross and being wrongfully murdered, his prayer was offering forgiveness to the very people killing him. This is where we have a tendency to sin even if we didn't do anything wrong.

When I found out that my dog had been murdered, it hurt a lot. It still hurts. But one thing I have to do is forgive the person who did this. If I don't, the Bible is clear that I won't be forgiven. But you see, when you've experienced the true forgiveness of Jesus, it's easy to forgive others, because you know that you've already been forgiven a tremendous debt! So my salvation is not dependent on my ability to forgive. I forgive because I've already been forgiven myself!

On September 6, 2018, twenty-six-year-old Botham Jean was home alone in his apartment when the door suddenly opened. To his surprise, it was a female police officer named Amber Guyger of the Dallas Police Department who just finished a 13.5-hour shift. As it turns out, Amber lived in the apartment one floor below Botham. However, Amber believed that as she opened the door, she was entering her own apartment. Alarmed that somebody was in her apartment (or so she thought), Amber retrieved her gun and shot Botham Jean, killing him. Amber's mistake cost an innocent man his life. In fact, how much more innocent can you get than just being home alone in your apartment? As you can expect, the family of Botham was absolutely distraught. Their loved one was taken because of a police officer's negligence. In the coming days, the family voiced their hatred for Amber Guyger, even calling her the devil. It's hard to imagine the anger this family felt over this tragic mistake.

After a lengthy trial, on October 1, 2019, Amber Guyger was found guilty of murder and was sentenced to ten years in prison. Some of the family members were then given a chance to address Amber and express the hole in their life that her actions caused. One of the family members was Botham's young brother, Brandt, who was eighteen years old.

As Brandt began attempting to formulate his emotions into words, here's what he said:

> I don't want to say twice or for the hundredth time what you've…or how much you've taken from us. I think you know that. But I just…I hope you go to God, with all the guilt, all the bad things you may have done in the past. Each and every one of us may have done something that we're not supposed to do. If you truly are sorry, I know, I can speak for myself, I forgive you. And I know if you go to God and ask him, he will forgive you. And I don't think anyone can say it—again I'm just speaking for myself, not even on behalf of my family—but I love you just like anyone else. And I'm not gonna say I hope you rot and die, just like my brother did, but I personally want the best for you. I wasn't ever gonna say this in front of my family or anyone, but I don't even want you to go to jail. I want the best for you, because I know that's exactly what Botham would want you to do. And the best would be, give your life to Christ. I'm not gonna say anything else. I think giving your life to Christ would be the best thing that Botham would want you to do. Again, I love you as a person, and I don't wish anything bad on you.

After concluding his statement, Brandt asked the judge for permission to hug Amber, and the two embraced and cried with each other, displaying an amazing amount of forgiveness. Forgiveness has an amazing way of making anger leave. Despite the wrong that had been done to Brandt, he chose to forgive, just like Jesus did.

Jesus and the Children

Another time when Jesus showed anger is when he saw kids getting looked down upon. Matthew, Mark, and Luke all record an event where kids were being brought to Jesus and his own disciples tried to stop it from happening! In the disciples' minds, Jesus was too busy to consider the needs of children. In Mark's Gospel, it says that Jesus saw this happening and he was indignant. Indignant is a great word to describe Jesus's emotion in this situation because being indignant means to be angry or annoyed at what is perceived as unfair treatment. When Jesus saw that the children were treated this way, he felt that this was unfair. Mark 10:14–16 records Jesus saying:

> 'Let the little children come to me, and do not hinder them, for the kingdom of God belongs to such as these. Truly I tell you, anyone who will not receive the kingdom of God like a little child will never enter it.' And he took the children in his arms, placed his hands on them, and blessed them.

It's a nice story, and it's very reassuring that Jesus was so kind to the children that he defended them. But think about what Jesus said or, more importantly, what he didn't say. He was angry at this treatment of children and he spoke up! He didn't just let it slide in order to be peaceful. However, even in his anger, he didn't sin. It would have been easy for Jesus to cross a line and start attacking the disciples' character, hurl insults at them, and possibly call them names. But Jesus didn't do any of those. He addressed the matter in a way that affirmed the kids, and he didn't let his anger lead him to sin.

When I'm wronged, I tend to exaggerate. I remember getting a bad grade in seminary on a book report. When I filled out the review for the professor at the end of the semester, I did not hold back from attacking him. I felt that since he had given me a bad grade unfairly, he needed to be attacked as a person. I wrote about his personal life and how he probably lived alone and found his only pleasure in giving bad grades on papers. Don't get me wrong, he definitely gave me an unfair grade, and I had a legitimate reason to be angry. However, I crossed the line and let my anger lead me to sin. For that, I am guilty before God with no excuse and no one to blame but myself.

Jesus's example on how to deal with anger is brilliant. In every situation, his anger is justified because of the unfair treatment that he sees. He's bold enough to confront the wrong yet does this without taking things too far and allowing sin to take place. This is the exact command we have from Ephesians 4:25–27, which says:

> Therefore each of you must put off falsehood and speak truthfully to your neighbor, for we are all members of one body. 'In your anger do not sin': Do not let the sun go down while you are still angry, and do not give the devil a foothold.

Later in Ephesians 4, it says to get rid of anger. Anger is not something that we should hold on to. There may be a time to be angry, but we are told to not let the sun go down while we're still angry. We should follow Jesus's example and not hold on to it longer than we should.

It shouldn't shock us that Jesus got angry on occasion. We know that Jesus is fully God, and God shows his anger and wrath against sin multiple times throughout scripture. Look up the phrase, "The anger of the Lord burned," and look at all the instances that come up from the Old Testament when God was angry. The God of the Old Testament is the same God of the New Testament. His heart, character, and love for justice and mercy is unchanging. The thing that makes God angry is sin. And when Jesus saw the sin that was taking place at the temple, his anger burned.

Do you struggle with anger? I hear a lot of students talk about the circumstances with their parents, friends, and teachers, and they always seem to chalk up their conflict to their anger issues. Listen, anger isn't a sin. The question, though, is what are you getting angry about? Jesus didn't really get angry about personal attacks or things that were trivial. Think about his reaction when people were talking bad about him in Matthew 15, as we discussed in chapter 4. He let them talk about him without feeling the need to put them in their place. Jesus got mad when he saw people and people groups being treated unfairly. And when he did display anger, he never allowed it to lead him to sin. If you struggle with anger in unnecessary circumstances, ask God to start making you angry for righteous things instead of trivial things. Follow Jesus's example and stand up for people when they are being mistreated, but do it according to God's Word. And no matter what, be quick to forgive.

Slow to Anger

We also must point out that even though the Bible talks about God's anger on several occasions, it also tells us that he's slow to anger. Exodus 34:6; Numbers 14:18; Nehemiah 9:17; Psalm 86:15; Psalm 103:8; Psalm 145:8; Joel 2:13; and Jonah 4:2 all mention a phrase that God is *slow to anger and abounding in steadfast love.* Proverbs 14:29 says, "Whoever is slow to anger has great understanding, but he who has a hasty temper exalts folly." Similarly, Proverbs 19:11 says, "Good sense makes one slow to anger, and it is his glory to overlook an offense." Don't miss this! You have permission to overlook offenses. If you are able to learn how to overlook offenses, it will be to your glory! While you may be wronged from time to time, you have permission to overlook the offense and to be slow to anger. This is certainly lost in our culture today. For a Christian striving to become more like Jesus, our goal is not to react to circumstances the way that the rest of the world does, but to be different.

There is a biographical film titled *End of the Spear* that was released in 2005. The film retells the real life story of five American Christian missionaries who went out to preach the gospel to the Waodani people in the rainforest of Eastern Ecuador. After making contact with the Waodani people, misinformation was spread about the missionaries, and warriors from the Waodani tribe killed the five missionaries by spearing them to death. Years later, a man named Steve Saint, who was the son of one of the missionaries who was murdered, flew into Ecuador and ended up meeting a warrior from the Waodani tribe named Mincayani. Steve and Mincayani formed a friendship, and one day, Mincayani took Steve on a canoe to show him where his father had been speared to death. When they arrived at the location, Mincayani revealed that he was the one who killed Steve's father unjustly. At that moment, Mincayani gave Steve a spear and told him to kill him to atone for his father's death. Steve now had an opportunity to get even for his father's murder. Instead, he forgave Mincayani and said, "My father didn't lose his life, he gave his life." Steve continued to live among the Waodani people and spread the gospel. His life was a living example of what it looks like to overlook an offense and forgive. The Waodani people got to see the love of Jesus through the life of Steve.

Conclusion

There are times when we have every right to be angry. When angry, having the patience to slow down like Jesus did is a good start. We should ask ourselves if we have a biblical right to be angry, but we also get the choice of what we're going to do with our anger. Not all anger is the same. There are going to be times when we need to be bold and defend others and stand up for truth. There are other times when we have the chance to overlook an offense. Whatever the case, our actions should always be done in a way that enhances the Kingdom of God. The actions of Steve Saint did. The actions of Brandt Jean did. And the actions of Jesus certainly did. There is a time to be angry and a time to let it go.

CHAPTER 9

What Did Jesus Do with Evangelism?

**But in your hearts revere Christ as Lord. Always
be prepared to give an answer to everyone who
asks you to give the reason for the hope that you
have. But do this with gentleness and respect.**
—1 Peter 3:15 NIV

Up to this point in our discussion, we've examined how Jesus handled common issues that we all face from time to time in life. You may have struggled in one or two of the areas or maybe you're like me and everything we've talked about has been an issue at some point in life. You may be curious about the title of this chapter. Sure, it's easy to struggle with temptation or anger, but how do you struggle with evangelism? What even is evangelism?

Evangelism is the spreading of the gospel. The gospel is the good news of the kingdom of God and that Jesus is the king in this kingdom who has come to take away the sins of the world. Christians have a call from scripture to spread this good news and win the whole world to Christ. If you're reading this book as a Christian, you have a responsibility of evangelism. That is, spreading the gospel. One of the most sinful and God-hating places you can go to is school. In most cases, the number of unsaved kids and teachers in your school is greater than we care to acknowledge. Schools are saturated with teenagers who are heavily influenced by ungodly social media pages, and they so easily become obsessed with following the culture and doing whatever it takes to fit in and be cool. This quickly leads to perverse language, all kinds of smoking, many sexual relationships, and an overall hatred for the God who created them and gives them air to breathe.

As a Christian, we recognize this is the lost world that Jesus has called us to reach. Matthew 28:18–20 says:

> All authority in heaven and on earth has been given to me. Therefore go and make disciples of all nations, baptizing them in the name of the Father and of the Son and of the Holy Spirit, and teaching them to obey everything I have commanded you. And surely I am with you always, to the very end of the age.

Interestingly enough, these are the last words that Jesus says before ascending into heaven. After everything that Jesus has been through and everything that he has taught his disciples, the last words he says to them are the command to take this good news out and make disciples of all nations. The Apostle Paul elaborates on this idea in 2 Corinthians 5:18–20 by writing:

> God, who reconciled us to himself through Christ and gave us the ministry

of reconciliation: that God was reconcil-
ing the world to himself in Christ, not
counting people's sins against them. And
he has committed to us the message of
reconciliation. We are therefore Christ's
ambassadors, as though God were making his appeal through us.

This is absolutely fascinating and mind blowing! The
eternal God, who created the entire universe, reconciled
us to himself and now has committed to us the message of
reconciliation. That means that he's given us the job to go
out and be ambassadors for him, realizing that God is using
us, mere humans, to reconcile more people to himself. In
1 Corinthians 3, Paul actually goes as far to say that we're
coworkers with God. What an honor to be used by God to
accomplish his purposes!

This means that even if you haven't thought of evangelism as something that you need to know about or should
be participating in, it's actually commanded by God that we
do it. The truth is, most of you don't have to look far to
find unbelieving friends. We all have a circle of people that
we interact with in some way, and within our circle, there
are more than likely unbelievers here or there. They may
be atheists, followers of man-made religions, or professing
Christians who don't act like Christians at all. Whatever the
case, the call of the Scriptures is for true Christians to spread
the gospel and reach these unbelievers.

This can be a daunting task! It's easy to feel unpre-
pared or underqualified to be telling others what they should
believe. It's easier to leave that job to preachers and worship
leaders. At our very best, we might feel comfortable invit-

ing someone to church. But actually telling somebody about Jesus? That seems hard to do.

I remember when I was sixteen years old, and I got my driver's license. I was so excited to be able to drive myself without any supervision. My parents had given me a 2005 Ford Focus. It wasn't the nicest car in the world, but I didn't care! I had a car that was mine, and I felt pretty confident driving my little Ford Focus around. The week after I got my license, a single mom at our church who had two young kids called me and said she was moving. She asked if I would be able to help since I just got my driver's license. I was more than happy to help out. She was in a desperate situation, and I kind of enjoyed getting to put my car and driver's license to use. So I met her over at her apartment. She had rented a large U-Haul. The kind that you drive similar to a small 18-wheeler. We loaded up the U-Haul with all of the furniture from her old apartment, and it was time to head to the new apartments to unload all of the furniture out of the U-Haul. It was at this moment that the unexpected happened. She handed me the keys to this ginormous U-Haul and told me to follow her to the new apartment. As I was taking the keys from her hands, I had a knot in my throat, my hands started to sweat, and I felt like I might throw up right there. You see, I've been driving for about eight and a half days. I'm fairly comfortable driving my little Focus, but you expect me to know how to drive this beast of a car? I acted like I knew this was the plan all along, but in reality, I was scared to death to drive this huge thing! That's a lot of responsibility, and I didn't want to run anyone over!

We started the journey to the new apartment, and thankfully, I made it to the apartment with only a few people honking at me. It wasn't the smoothest drive, but I didn't cause any accidents. We pulled in the parking lot, and I felt like I was out of the woods and a weight was lifted off me. But once we pulled around to where her new apartment was, there were cars everywhere! She parked and walked over to me and gave me instructions to back into an extremely tight space that was surrounded by cars. I'll be completely honest, I had no idea what I was doing! As I began maneuvering this giant U-Haul around, I somehow ended up getting it in such a predicament that if I made any other move, I was going to hit another car. To make matters worse, everybody was watching! People in other apartments even started looking out of their windows to see what was going to happen. I got out of the U-Haul, and I said, "Let's just knock on some doors, and tell whoever to come move their car so that I don't hit any of them."

The lady then replied, "That's okay. I can get out of this."

She then proceeds to get in the U-Haul and back it up. When she began backing up, the corner of the U-Haul made contact with another car and lifted it off the ground! My worst nightmare had become a reality. People started yelling and calling the cops. I felt like I had committed a heinous crime. I honestly just wanted to sit down under a tree and die.

See, I was given the big responsibility to drive the U-Haul, but I didn't know how to drive the U-Haul. Likewise, sharing the gospel with our friends, neighbors, and community is a big responsibility. The biggest thing that keeps us from doing it is that we don't know how to share the gospel. And we end up looking like sixteen-year-old Evan driving the U-Haul. It's not a pretty picture.

Most Christians believe we should follow the big commands from scripture such as loving our neighbor or honoring our parents. I agree with this. But believe it or not, there is actually a command in scripture to be prepared to defend the faith. In 1 Peter 3:15, it says:

> In your hearts revere Christ as Lord.
> Always be prepared to give an answer to
> everyone who asks you to give the reason
> for the hope that you have. But do this
> with gentleness and respect.

Similarly, Jude 3 states that we are to "contend earnestly for the faith that was once for all time handed down to the saints" (NASB). Evangelism can seem like a task that we leave for theologians and scholars since they might actually know what they're talking about. The reality is, all Christians are called to evangelize and to contend for the faith.

Using Words

How do we handle this responsibility? A large portion of the American church has saturated Christians with beliefs about evangelism that are incompatible with the example that we have from scripture. Many of us have grown up hearing and believing such things that we think they're grounded in biblical truth, when in fact, they are not. The belief system is that rather than telling the story of the gospel, we should just be really good Christians and let other people take notice. Many Christians teach that instead of telling someone about Jesus, we should be Jesus to them and that we may be the only Jesus that someone ever meets. First of all, this is not what the scriptures teach. Romans 1 claims that there is enough revelation just in the creation alone that everybody knows God, and they are without excuse for their rejection of him. But secondly, if there were a person who never heard or encountered Jesus in any way other than looking at the way I live my life, that would be bad news for this person. I'm so far from perfect and so far away from being anything close to Jesus. The true Jesus saves people, not someone seeing the way I live my life. I am a sinner and was dead in my sins. God has been rich in mercy and has saved me so that I can have peace with him, but he has so much more work to do in me to make me like Jesus. My example in life will never make someone else a Christian. In fact, the hard reality to accept is that nobody will accept Jesus as their Lord and Savior by seeing the way you live.

Now don't set out to prove me wrong just yet! Let me explain. I am well aware of what Jesus says in Matthew 5:16 when he says, "Let your light shine before others, that they may see your good deeds and glorify your Father in heaven." So I'm not saying that you shouldn't let your light shine before men or that you shouldn't strive to be like Jesus. Rather, I am making the argument that the apostles who heard this message firsthand did not understand it to mean that we should let our light shine by being nice to people but not actually telling them the good news of the kingdom with our words.

When the Apostle Paul became a Christian after encountering Jesus in Acts 9, the first thing he did was use his words to preach the gospel. Acts 9:20–22 explains it this way:

> At once he began to preach in the synagogues that Jesus is the Son of God. All those who heard him were astonished and asked, "Isn't he the man who raised havoc in Jerusalem among those who call on this name? And hasn't he come here to take them as prisoners to the chief priests?" Yet Saul grew more and more

powerful and baffled the Jews living in Damascus by proving that Jesus is the Messiah.

Did you catch that? He proved that Jesus was the Messiah. We are told that Apollos does the same thing in Acts 18:28 as it says, "He vigorously refuted his Jewish opponents in public debate, proving from the Scriptures that Jesus was the Messiah." Couple these examples with Peter and Jude's claim that we ought to be ready to defend the faith, and it's clear that using our words is essential in the spreading of the gospel.

Sadly, the American church tends to think the exact opposite. One famous saying that has become popular and often gets reposted around on social media is this: "Always preach the gospel, and when necessary, use words." Greg Stier comments on this phrase, saying:

> I cringe when I hear it. The apostle Paul wouldn't have liked it either. I changed it to, "Preach the gospel. It's necessary. Use words."

We would never say, "Always feed the hungry, and when necessary, use food." It doesn't make any sense! I recently read a tweet from a prominent pastor that said, "The best evangelism is always done without ever saying a word." This is not the example we see from the apostles in the slightest degree. In response to this tweet, Pastor Jeff Durbin of Apologia Church writes:

> This is modern "Evangelical" foolishness. There is no "evangel" (Gospel/

Good News) without words. Have you ever received "news" without words and communication? This is why we are ineffective and have lost the clarity of the Gospel in this generation. We don't "Gospel" like Jesus and the Apostles.

The Gospel comes as a command to repent and believe. The Gospel tells a story about our sin and the identity and work of the Messiah. The sooner we abandon this kind of weak-kneed, ignorant, and cowardly drivel the better for actual lost people. God help us.

Think about how you feel when you hear good news. I remember the moment Haley told me she was pregnant with our daughter, Zoe. I was so excited I could hardly contain myself. I was putting my shoes on so that we could go tell our families this wonderful news! Haley had to slow me down and explain that it might be best to wait a few weeks until we can go to the doctor to confirm. But I couldn't wait. I convinced Haley that we should tell our families the next day. The news was just too good to keep to myself! How silly would it be to hold the good news in and hope that our families learned of the good news by our actions? That's ridiculous! It may not happen all the time, but when we receive good news, we want to tell somebody!

Why then, has it become standard practice among American Christians to stop using our words to spread the gospel? It's the same reason for my writing of this book. We have a tendency to ignore the examples and commands from scripture, and we bend to what seems to be most acceptable. The reality is that there is a lost world that desperately needs to hear the gospel. Romans 10:14 says, "How can they believe in the one of whom they have not heard? And how can they hear without someone preaching to them?" As the Apostle Paul is writing this, he clearly has in his mind that unbelievers need to hear the gospel! The only way they can hear is if someone is using their words to proclaim it.

The apostles clearly have a different view on evangelism than the current American culture does, but what about Jesus? What did he do with evangelism? Wouldn't it be kind of weird to go around and tell people to believe in himself? The cool thing is, we have examples from scripture of what Jesus did with evangelism.

Repent and Believe!

For whatever reason, some people often correct others on what Jesus would do without even using scripture to back up their claims. It's as if they have a view of Jesus in their minds and assume that's what he's like in the Bible. I tend to wonder if these people ever read their Bibles at all.

In Mark's account of the life of Jesus, the first words that he records Jesus saying are in Mark 1:15 when Jesus says, "The time has come," he said. "The kingdom of God has come near. Repent and believe the good news!" How crazy is that? The very first words that Mark records Jesus saying is actually him using his words to proclaim the gospel. Later on in Mark 1, he answers his disciples and says, "Let us go somewhere else—to the nearby villages—so I can preach there also. That is why I have come." Jesus said that he wanted to go to the nearby villages to preach the gospel. Notice what he didn't say. He didn't say that he wanted to go to the nearby villages to be nice to people and do good things to see if they ask him why he's so nice and then hope for a chance to share the good news of the kingdom. Instead, he wants to go preach! Preaching involves words just like eating involves food. Jesus goes as far to say that the preaching of the good news of the kingdom is why he has come!

Matthew 9:35 says, "Jesus went through all the towns and villages, teaching in their synagogues, proclaiming the good news of the kingdom and healing every disease and sickness." I would say that healing every disease and sickness is a nice thing to do. Whether you have a chronic illness or a little headache, you're going to be thankful for being healed! Jesus was nice. But he didn't let his good deeds be the sole motivating factor for people to learn about the kingdom of God. He taught in the synagogues, and he proclaimed the good news. The only way to proclaim something is with your words, and that's the example we have from Jesus.

Because of His Words

Not every encounter that Jesus had with people consisted of him bluntly telling them to repent and believe. Remember, Jesus was a human, not a robot. John 4 records a famous story of Jesus having a conversation with a Samaritan woman at a well. The conversation starts out simple by Jesus asking the woman for a drink from the well. This shocked the woman because she was a Samaritan and Jesus was Jewish, and those cultures weren't supposed to interact with each other. She even asks him how he could make that request in light of their nationalities. In this moment, Jesus takes an ordinary conversation and begins to tell this woman some good news. In verse 10, Jesus responds to her question about how he can ask her for water by saying, "If you knew the gift of God and who it is that asks you for a drink, you would have asked him and he would have given you living water."

He then explains that everyone who drinks the living water will never be thirsty again. For a woman who has to work really hard to get water every day by travelling far and carrying the heavy buckets all the way back, the idea that there is a living water that will satisfy her thirst is pretty enticing. So she asks for Jesus to give her this living water!

The conversation then leads to Jesus pointing out some things in her life, and she concludes that Jesus must be a prophet. When the woman is confused about the details of their conversation, she says that "I know that Messiah (called Christ) is coming. When he comes, he will explain everything to us." Finally, Jesus reveals to the woman that he is the Messiah that she's expecting.

This is an intriguing encounter that Jesus has and there are a lot of conclusions that we can draw. But how could we model this type of evangelism? We can't tell people their past like Jesus could. We can't physically show someone the Messiah like Jesus did. So what can we learn from this encounter? Think about all the ordinary conversations we have every day. Maybe it's with the neighbor as we're checking the mail, maybe with a teammate in the locker room, or maybe even with the waiter at a restaurant. Ordinary conversations present themselves all the time. How often do we have it in our mind to insert the gospel into our conversations? If you read John 4 for yourself, you'll notice that Jesus doesn't feel any awkwardness. He certainly doesn't hesitate or dance around the truth by saying something like, "I'm not trying to tell you what to believe in" or "Everybody has their own opinion." Rather, he boldly and humbly explained to the woman the thing that will truly satisfy in life. That is, the living water.

I don't want to read something into the passage that's not true, but it doesn't seem like Jesus went to that well for the sole purpose of getting water. Sure, he may have been thirsty.

But I think the conversation with the woman was his main reason for showing up at the well. In fact, the woman went and told the people in her town about her conversation with her, and it says that many of them believed in Jesus because of the woman's testimony, and they urged Jesus to stay with them for a while. Jesus ended up staying with them for two days, and verse 41 says, "And because of his words many more became believers." Wow! The conversation that Jesus had with this one individual woman led to many non-Jewish people becoming believers. Why did they become believers? Because of *his words.*

Jesus knew that his purpose for coming to earth was to preach the gospel. Is that the purpose that we wake up with every day? Are we looking for opportunities to share the gospel like Jesus did? It wasn't just in the public preaching that Jesus shared the good news. It was also in the individual conversations that he pursued.

Contending for faith isn't only done with atheists or people who claim to have no belief system. It should also be done with people who follow man-made religions. The vocabulary of people who belong to man-made religions oftentimes sounds very Christian. They will say the same words that Christians say, and on the surface, it can be hard to tell a difference between true Christianity and a man-made version. Some of these man-made religions that I am referring to would be the Church of Jesus Christ of Latter-Day Saints (Mormonism), the Watchtower Tract Society (Jehovah's Witnesses), World Mission Society Church of God, Seventh-Day Adventist, Christian Science, and on and on. My hope is to one day write a book describing the differences between these religions in detail and equipping true Christians on how to evangelize these groups with the true gospel. While you may not be an expert on the differences right now, I want to show you a texting conversation I had with a Mormon friend of mine. Here's how it went:

> Mormon: You have a lot of faith, as with many believers in Jesus Christ. Ultimately it comes down to faith, wouldn't you say?
>
> Me: Absolutely. But faith has to be in the right God and the right gospel. In 2 Corinthians 11:3–4, Paul is worried that the Corinthians will accept a different Jesus or a different gospel. You might ask, "How can there be a different Jesus?" The answer is that different people teach different versions of him. And if you have faith in the wrong Jesus, he can't save you.
>
> Mormon: And the Jesus I believe in can't save me? So as of right now, I'm not saved?
>
> Me: Joseph Smith (who is the founder of the Mormon church) teaches that Jesus is Lucifer's brother. The Bible teaches that Jesus is the creator of everything, which would include Lucifer, you, and me. That's a different Jesus.
>
> Mormon: Okay I see what you mean. So question, if I continue living this way will I go to hell?

Here is where I have the opportunity to be cordial and continue our friendship or risk it all and love him enough to tell him the truth. Here is what I said:

> Me: That's my great concern for you, yes.
> Mormon: I do nothing wrong though! I live a good life, I serve, I read my scriptures, I pray, I love my parents…even with all this, I'm going to hell? I know I still make mistakes, I try to be better though.

This is exactly why it is necessary for us to evangelize to our friends and neighbors. This young man has grown up in a church that has taught him that being a good person can earn him peace with God. He just has to be good. There's a major problem though. Romans 3:12 says that "there is none good, not even one." Jesus even says that only God is good. Paul writes in Galatians 5:4, "You who are trying to be justified by the law have been alienated from Christ; you have fallen away from grace." This young man has been taught that his good deeds can earn him peace with God. If a true Christian won't love him enough to explain the true gospel to him, who will? Who's going to be the one who shares the gospel with your atheist friend at school? Who's going to share the gospel with your friend who is all wrapped up in sin? What about your parents? Do they need the gospel? Being a nice person without speaking the truth won't lead someone to Christ. The truth is, some of the nicest people on the planet are my Mormon friends. If somebody is drawn to their love, they're going to be drawn to a false Christ and a false gospel.

Conclusion

The world we live in certainly wants us to think that everybody is entitled to their own opinion and that everyone can have their own truth. People certainly have their opinions and their beliefs, but we, by no means, should sit by silently while the lost world around us perishes. In Acts 5, Peter and some other disciples have been warned to stop speaking about Jesus. Peter's response in verse 29 is spot on. He says, "We must obey God rather than human beings!" The pressure to stay silent about our faith is certainly still prevalent today. The sad thing is, even a large portion of the American church encourages Christians to be silent too. Our question in this book has not been, "What do most Christians do?" Nor is it, "What is socially acceptable today?" The question is, "What did Jesus do?" He gave us a crystal-clear example of how evangelism should be done and it is unquestionably to be done with words, proclaiming that the kingdom of heaven is here. Jesus was humble, bold, and direct.

Whether or not a person comes to faith in Christ because of our engagement with them is not for us to worry about. Our job as God's coworkers is to spread the message of reconciliation, knowing that God is the one who reconciles people to himself. The cool thing is that when you get passionate about evangelism, it becomes contagious. Other Christians start to get inspired, and it sets off a chain reaction. At the same time, if you take this chapter to heart and begin living a life on mission to reach others with the gospel, you'll certainly get pushback from some. Will you obey God or human beings? Peter's answer was clear. Will ours be?

CHAPTER 10

What Did Jesus Accomplish?

**I am the Alpha and the Omega, the First and
the Last, the Beginning and the End.**
—Revelation 22:13 NIV

One of my favorite things to do with my friends growing up was riding bikes. When I was a teenager, my friends and I would ride our bikes all over the city. We would ride to the park, to the beach, and even to church. We weren't old enough to drive yet, so if we wanted to go somewhere, bikes were our best form of transportation. A guy at our church started noticing that we would ride bikes to church fairly often, and so one day, he asked me if I would ever be interested in competing in a triathlon. To be honest, I had no clue what a triathlon even was, but it sounded like a challenge, so I was all for it. He explained to me that it was a race that involved 500 meters of swimming, a 15-mile bike ride, and then a 3.1-mile run. With as good of shape I was in from all of the bike riding, I knew I would be able to make it through this race.

The first thing this guy told me was that I was going to need to purchase a road bike. I laughed at him when he told me that. I mean, come on. I ride my bike all over this city. Why wouldn't I be able to ride it in this triathlon? He convinced me to go on a training ride with him, and boy was I wrong. The difference between riding around the city for fun and competing in a race is night and day. I had to admit that I was wrong, and I saved up money to buy a new road bike. Thank goodness I did. After barely surviving the swim portion of the race, the bike portion was way harder than I expected it to be. Reality began to set in that I may not have been in quite as good of shape as I thought I was. The route for the bike portion was on the seawall of the beach, and the wind was blowing as if there was a hurricane approaching. I felt like I had been riding for so long when I saw a sign that said, "Mile 3." That was the most disheartening sign I've ever seen. I figured we were probably on mile 9 or 10 at this point. But only mile 3? I started to wonder if I was gonna be able to make it through this race.

When I first arrived at the triathlon, I noticed they wrote the age of everyone on the back of their leg so that you could see what age group you're competing against during the race. I was getting passed by people of all ages. It started to hurt my feelings and my legs when I would see people in their seventies pass me. But then everything took a turn for the worse. I noticed a girl was passing me. I looked at her age on the back of her leg and my heart sank. She was seven... years...old. I'm a fifteen-year-old guy struggling so bad that a little girl was able to pass me. Not to mention that the girls started ten minutes after the guys started. About that time, a seventy-six-year-old man passed me and asked, "You doing okay, youngster?"

I was way too out of breath to respond, but if I could have, I probably would have said, "You know what, no! I'm not okay! I just got passed by a seven-year-old girl. Things are obviously not okay!"

Somehow, someway, I made it through the biking portion. The thought of running at all was incredibly intimidating, yet alone running three miles!

But I had to start somewhere, so I started putting one foot in front of the other. After I ran the world's slowest mile, I realized my shoe was untied. I ignored it for a little while. To this day, I remember the race number I was wearing, because a lady screamed it at me as I ran by saying, "976, your shoe!"

I bent down to tie it and when I did, both of my legs started cramping up to the point that I didn't think I would be able to keep running. Once again though, I just started putting one foot in front of the other. By the grace of God, I made it across the finish line. Since that day, I've completed several more triathlons and races after training properly. But looking back at that first one, I remember how hard it was. In hindsight, some of the memories make me laugh. I remember my friends being worried about me being able to make it to the car because I didn't think I could walk anymore. I certainly didn't win that race, but that hard day would have been all for nothing if I didn't finish. Finishing the triathlon was an accomplishment that I could celebrate and be proud of myself for. Had I not finished, that day would have been an utter failure.

The Rescue for Sinners

When we look at the example of Jesus, it's important to remember the reason he came. In Luke 19:10, Jesus says, "For the Son of Man came to seek and to save the lost." In Mark 10:45, he says, "For even the Son of Man did not come to be served, but to serve, and to give his life as a ransom for many." Finally, in John 18:37, Jesus says, "You say that I am a king. In fact, the reason I was born and came into the world is to testify to the truth. Everyone on the side of truth listens to me." Jesus is pretty clear on his reason for coming to earth. He came to rescue sinners. If he were to come to earth and teach us all of this great wisdom on how we ought to live and if he modeled it by giving us a perfect example, but didn't accomplish what he came to do, it would all be for nothing. In fact, if Jesus didn't die for sins and defeat death by rising again, he would be nothing more than a prophet. That sounds a lot like the Jesus of Islam. They respect him as a prophet, but they don't believe he died for sins.

If we only view the life of Jesus as a means to learn how we should live, then we've missed the point altogether. Don't get me wrong, it's amazing that we can look at the way in which Jesus lived his life and how he handled circumstances and emotions and learn from those things ourselves. But he's not just our example, he's our savior and king. And the call of the gospel is not only to become like Jesus in certain areas of our lives, it's to completely surrender our lives altogether and make him the Lord of our lives. As previously mentioned, Jesus says in Matthew 10:37–38:

> Anyone who loves their father or mother more than me is not worthy of me; anyone who loves their son or daughter more than me is not worthy of me. Whoever does not take up their cross and follow me is not worthy of me.

According to Jesus, following him requires everything. We have a tendency to treat Jesus as somebody that we believe in, and sometimes, we become content with that.

The culture we live in sells us on the desperate need to be known and leave a legacy. We get laser focused on these things and we do whatever it takes to achieve them. The number of likes we get on Instagram or the number of views we get on TikTok tend to define us, and we're always chasing more. Being popular, getting a nice car, and the best-looking girl are some of the things that become essential for us. As you get older, having a respectable career that pays well becomes one of the major motivators in life. Then it's all about having a family, buying a house, then buying a bigger house, and somewhere along the way, Jesus just becomes a part of our life instead of our whole life. We believe in him so that we can go to heaven one day, but we don't necessarily live every day as if he's the king of our life, and we certainly don't recognize his authority on the earth.

A Ticket to Heaven?

This sort of lifestyle where Jesus becomes a ticket to heaven instead of Lord of all is displayed in Matthew 19. This portion of scripture is a conversation between a rich young man and Jesus. It is extraordinarily important to understand this passage, so let's go through it verse by verse. It begins with the rich young man asking Jesus a question in Matthew 19:16. He asks, "Teacher, what good thing must I do to get eternal life?" The young man begins the conversation by asking a question that proves he doesn't understand the gospel at all. He's asking what good thing he needs to do in order to go to heaven when he dies. This is a question that a lot of people ask. The truth is, there is no good thing that one can do to get eternal life. Jesus begins to answer this in verse 17 when he replies, "Why do you ask me about what is good?" There is only One who is good. If you want to enter life, keep the commandments." First of all, Jesus mentions that there is only One who is good. The implication is that God is the one who is good. What does this mean about Jesus? Isn't he good? Of course, he is. That makes Jesus, God. He then tells the young man that if he wants to enter into life, to keep the commandments to which the young man replies, "Which ones?" And Jesus said, "You shall not murder, you shall not commit adultery, You shall not steal, You shall not bear false witness, Honor your father and mother, and, You shall love your neighbor as yourself" (Matt. 19:18–19). Jesus says plainly that he didn't come to abolish the law, but to fulfill it (Matt. 5:17). Therefore, when telling the young man what to do for life, he simply points back to the law. Yet Jesus knows that the conversation will not end here.

Verse 20 says, "The young man said to him, 'All these I have kept. What do I still lack?'" As Jesus already knew, the young man is feeling a sense that keeping the commandments isn't going to be enough to save him. And he would be right. The law cannot save people and it never could. God has always saved people by grace alone as Romans 3 and 4 points out. Jesus then tells the young man what attaining eternal life will require. He says, "If you would be perfect, go, sell what you possess and give to the poor, and you will have treasure in heaven; and come, follow me" (Matt 19:21). This is where many people get it wrong. Jesus says time and time again what it costs to follow him. It costs everything. We must be willing to lose everything for the sake of following Jesus. For people who only wish to believe in Jesus as a means to get into heaven, this is a hard pill to swallow. It's clearly hard for the young man, as verse 22 says, "When the young man heard this he went away sorrowful, for he had great possessions." When the young man learns that giving up his life to follow Jesus is the way to eternal life, he weighs the costs and realizes he would rather have his temporary wealth than eternal life. Realistically, Jesus was only helping this young man see that he didn't actually want to follow Jesus, he only wanted a free ticket to heaven. Jesus already said in Matthew 6:24, "No one can serve two masters, for either he will hate the one and love the other, or he will be devoted to the one and despise the other. You cannot serve God and money." It wasn't the fact that he had stuff that prevented the young man from following Jesus. It was his devotion to his stuff. When given the choice between Jesus and his stuff, the young man chose his stuff.

It forces us to ask ourselves, "What are the things that have more of my devotion than Jesus?" It's a hard question to ask and the answer that we give ourselves might be even harder to accept. There's a large misconception among many of us that some people are just really in love with Jesus and so spending time with him is easy. They believe that these people find it so easy to pray regularly and to read large portions of scripture. I don't think it always comes easy though. There are always other things pulling us in different directions. But those who love Jesus recognize their desperate need for him and so spending time in prayer and reading the scriptures isn't optional. It's that or give in to other things that are begging for their devotion. And if there's one thing we can learn from the rich young man who chose his stuff over Jesus, it's that our stuff isn't worth it. Jesus says in Matthew 16:26, "For what will it profit a man if he gains the whole world and forfeits his soul? Or what shall a man give in return for his soul?" Anything we can attain on earth is worthless if it costs us our soul.

Justification and Sanctification

The truth is, trusting in Jesus for salvation is only the very beginning. It's certainly not just a free ticket to heaven. There are two fancy theological words called justification and sanctification. They sound complicated, but they're actually pretty simple. Justification is what takes place when we put our faith in Christ. In that moment, we are justified from our sin and made right with God, and this is an instantaneous thing. Oh, the amazing grace that Jesus displayed by becoming sin for us and dying the death that we deserve so that we can have peace with God! My hope and prayer is that we never grow complacent with this life-changing truth!

Sanctification, however, is not an instantaneous thing. It's a lifelong process. To be sanctified means to be made holy. The journey of becoming holy will lead us to become more like Jesus. While it's great to learn how Jesus handled peer pressure, rejection, or anger, we must realize that if Jesus is the Lord of our lives, he is worthy of everything. He's worthy of all our devotion and the call of the gospel is to lay down our lives and live for him in every area. The best way to become like Jesus and handle life's challenges the way that Jesus did is to lay down our lives and follow him. When he becomes the Lord of our lives, we'll start seeing the world the way that he sees it. In time, our natural response is going to be treating people and circumstances the way that Jesus did. That's the beauty of sanctification. We have peace with God through his work of justification, and now we are growing in holiness. We are a work in progress!

Establishing the Kingdom

Understanding the impact of what Jesus accomplished is hard to fathom. We get really excited about being justified and having peace with God so that we can have eternal life. Then we see our need to become more like Jesus as we are being sanctified. As glorious as these are, the truth is, Jesus accomplished much more than saving sinners. As we mentioned in the last chapter, his message to people in his earthly ministry was to repent because the kingdom of heaven was near. Christ establishing his kingdom on earth is the story of the gospels.

Interestingly enough, Jesus wasn't accomplishing something unheard of. He was accomplishing what had been prophesied for centuries. Way back in Genesis 49:10, we see a prophecy of one who will reign as it says:

> The scepter will not depart from Judah,
> nor the ruler's staff from between his feet,
> until he to whom it belongs shall come and
> the obedience of the nations shall be his.

We know that Jesus comes from the tribe of Judah. The prophecy wasn't just speaking of one who would come to save people. It was talking about one who would come and reign and have the obedience of the nations be his. God promises King David in 2 Samuel 7 that his kingdom will be an everlasting kingdom.

Psalm 2:7–8 says:

> I will proclaim the Lord's decree: He said
> to me, "You are my son; Today I have
> become your father. Ask me, and I will

make the nations your inheritance, the
ends of the earth your possession.

There are lots of interesting things to point out from Psalm 2. Notably, the inspired apostles in Acts 4 quote Psalm 2, and they make the claim that Psalm 2 is about Jesus. And he is promised the nations as his inheritance.

Psalm 110:1 is said to be God's favorite Bible verse as this is the most quoted Old Testament verse in the New Testament. It says, "The Lord says to my lord: 'Sit at my right hand until I make your enemies a footstool for your feet.'" This is obviously seen as a key verse in God's story since the New Testament quotes it and alludes to it repeatedly. My favorite prophecy about the future reign of the Messiah might just be Daniel 7:13–14. It says:

> I kept looking in the night visions, and
> behold, with the clouds of heaven one
> like a son of man was coming, and He
> came up to the Ancient of Days and was
> presented before Him. And to Him was
> given dominion, honor, and a kingdom,
> so that all the peoples, nations, and popu-
> lations of all languages might serve Him.
> His dominion is an everlasting dominion
> which will not pass away; and His king-
> dom is one which will not be destroyed.
> (NASB)

Notice what all of these passages have in common. They all talk about the future Messiah who is going to come and he's going to bring a kingdom and establish it. He's going to reign over his enemies, and all of the nations will obey him.

When Jesus is leaving earth and ascending into heaven, he actually tells his disciples that all authority in heaven and on earth has been given to him (Matt. 28:18). In other words, Jesus is now the King, and he is reigning over heaven and the earth. He accomplished what the Old Testament prophesied about all along. What an accomplishment!

Conclusion

My deepest hope is that by reading this book, you've learned to become more like Jesus. But even more than that, I hope your love for Jesus has grown and that you're convinced that he is worthy of everything we can offer. Jesus, being the reigning King, changes everything. He's in charge, he calls the shots, and he is going to put every enemy under his feet. The question is, do you simply believe in him, or is he ruling and reigning in your life? Today is the perfect day to dethrone whatever reigns in your life and submit to Jesus as king. We have no reason to fear the future or worry about what will become of us, we have a powerful king reigning and our job is only to trust and obey. It's so amazing that we are loved and chosen by the one who reigns! The almighty God, the King of kings, the promised Messiah, the Alpha and the Omega, the First and the Last, the Beginning and the End, the Lord of all.

So…what did Jesus do?

> Being in very nature God, he did not consider equality with God something to be used to his own advantage; rather, he made himself nothing by taking the very nature of a servant, being made in human likeness. And being found in appearance

as a man, he humbled himself by becoming obedient to death— even death on a cross!
Therefore God exalted him to the highest place and gave him the name that is above every name, that at the name of Jesus every knee should bow, in heaven and on earth and under the earth, and every tongue acknowledge that Jesus Christ is Lord, to the glory of God the Father. (Philippians 2:6–11)

The Lord reigns!